The Philosophy of Religion

First Books in Philosophy

Series Editor: Keith Yandell, University of Wisconsin-Madison

Blackwell's *First Books in Philosophy* series presents short, self-contained volumes which together provide a comprehensive introduction to the field. Each volume covers the major issues relevant to the subject at hand (e.g. philosophy of religion, ethics, philosophy of literature), and gives an account of the most plausible attempts to deal with the problems at hand.

Epistemology, Richard Fumerton

The Philosophy of Religion, Edward R. Wierenga

The Philosophy of Religion

Edward R. Wierenga

WILEY Blackwell

This edition first published 2016
© 2016 Edward R. Wierenga

Registered Office
John Wiley & Sons, Ltd, The Atrium, Southern Gate, Chichester, West Sussex, PO19 8SQ, UK

Editorial Offices
350 Main Street, Malden, MA 02148-5020, USA
9600 Garsington Road, Oxford, OX4 2DQ, UK
The Atrium, Southern Gate, Chichester, West Sussex, PO19 8SQ, UK

For details of our global editorial offices, for customer services, and for information about how to apply for permission to reuse the copyright material in this book please see our website at www.wiley.com/wiley-blackwell.

The right of Edward R. Wierenga to be identified as the author of this work has been asserted in accordance with the UK Copyright, Designs and Patents Act 1988.

Library of Congress Cataloging-in-Publication data applied for

9781405100878 [hardback]
9781405100885 [paperback]

A catalogue record for this book is available from the British Library.

Cover image: Chen Heng Kong / Shutterstock

Set in 10/12.5pt Galliard by SPi Global, Pondicherry, India
Printed and bound in Malaysia by Vivar Printing Sdn Bhd

1   2016

For Christina, Steve, and Kate

Contents

Preface

This book is an introduction to many of the leading topics in the philosophy of religion, including arguments for and against God's existence, the nature of several divine attributes, and the question of whether faith is rational in the absence of proof. It is intended for anyone who is interested in learning about issues and debates in the philosophy of religion. No previous exposure to philosophy is assumed, and more technical topics, such as how to evaluate arguments and how to think about metaphysical necessity and possibility, are introduced and explained before they are employed. Later chapters build on the methods introduced in earlier chapters, so readers with no prior study of philosophy are advised to start at the beginning. Although the book is intended to be introductory, I hope that there are enough original ideas or new ways of putting things to interest those already familiar with the field.

I believe that this book would also be useful in a course in philosophy of religion, either as the sole text or as a companion to one of the standard collections of historical and contemporary readings; for example, *Philosophy of Religion: An Anthology*, 7th edition (Rea and Pojman, 2015) or *Philosophy of Religion: Selected Readings*, 5th edition (Peterson, Hasker, Reichenbach, and Basinger, 2014).

I have benefited from several generations of students in my courses, whose questions and challenges have encouraged me to find clearer and more convincing ways of explaining things. I am grateful to Earl Conee and Richard Feldman for conversations on several of the topics of the book, especially, of course, on evidentialism in epistemology; and I am especially indebted to John G. Bennett and Todd Long, who generously provided insightful comments on a draft of the entire manuscript. The pervasive influence that the work of Alvin Plantinga has had on my philosophical thinking is displayed throughout the book, and I am happy to acknowledge his inspiration. Finally, I am grateful for a sabbatical leave for 2014–2015 from the University of Rochester, my academic home for the past 38 years, during which most of this book was written.

1

Introduction to the Philosophy of Religion

What is Philosophy of Religion?

Philosophy of religion is just thinking philosophically about topics that come up when the subject is religion. Thinking philosophically involves reflecting critically about a set of issues, with the aim of figuring out what to believe about those issues. Sometimes such reflection is simply about what we already believe. But open-minded inquiry requires reflecting, as well, on what others have thought, and it can involve examining proposals that no one else has articulated. One aspect of this kind of critical reflection may be illustrated by an anecdote about the comic actor, W. C. Fields (1880–1946), famous for playing somewhat mean-spirited and dissolute characters in what was apparently not casting against type. Near the end of his life, Fields was observed by a friend to be reading the Bible. Surprised, since Fields was not known to be at all religious, the friend asked, "What are you doing?" Field's reply, delivered in his characteristic snarl was, "Lookin' for loopholes, lookin' for loopholes."

Philosophers look for loopholes. They take details seriously, they subject claims to close scrutiny, and they try to find what's wrong with a given view. If the loophole they find is a (possibly made-up) case in which some general claim fails to hold, they have discovered a *counterexample*. Finding fault isn't the only thing philosophers do, however. For one thing, it's often not worth the trouble to look for loopholes to a claim that's too vague or too carelessly stated to tell exactly what it says. So another project in which philosophers engage is that of producing a careful and clear statement of the claim or thesis under consideration. This has the benefit of providing a clear target for scrutiny. But the very process of trying come up

The Philosophy of Religion, First Edition. Edward R. Wierenga.
© 2016 Edward R. Wierenga. Published 2016 by John Wiley & Sons, Ltd.

with a precise statement of a position often results in the discovery of complications or of needed distinctions that weren't apparent prior to attempting to state the position carefully. What emerges in this case is a deeper understanding of the complexity of the issues involved.

Another way in which philosophers try to introduce clarity before looking for loopholes is by carefully separating someone's reasons for holding a position from the position or thesis itself. Often the best way to do this is by constructing an argument for the thesis in question, with the reasons then being seen as the premises of this argument.[1] We'll look more closely at arguments later in this chapter. For now let's simply observe that disentangling a thesis from reasons for it, or a conclusion from the premises that are supposed to support it, gives us not only a clearer target to aim at but also opens up more possibilities for loopholes. As we'll see more precisely below, reasons can fail to be *good* reasons either by not being true or by failing to provide the right kind of support for the claim for which they are advanced. If we're serious about identifying a loophole in this kind of reasoning, we'll want to be able to say accurately what it is.

Finally, philosophers don't only set up targets for demolition. When a loophole is found, a constructive project is to attempt to fill it or to figure out a way to avoid the problem it has exposed. Perhaps a modest revision will escape the objection, or perhaps it would be better to look in a different direction altogether. Of course, any new proposal should be subjected to the same scrutiny that uncovered a flaw in the original proposal, and perhaps the new proposal will be found to have defects of its own. The process of looking for loopholes can have the felicitous outcome of leading to an improved formulation of a theory or claim, but even if it doesn't, it will lead to a greater understanding of what the issues are.

We've discussed in very general terms what it is to think philosophically, but we haven't looked at the second part of our subject: what is it to think philosophically *about religion*? One answer, in fact a pretty good answer, is that it is to employ the critical approach we have been discussing in the investigation of any topic that comes up when the subject is religion. As a matter of fact, philosophers of religion have found many such topics worth discussing. Some matters that we won't examine in this book include prayer, ritual, the nature of a saint, and defining religion, to mention just a few.

Instead, we'll take a cue from the fact that the major religions in the west – Judaism, Christianity, and Islam – are all *theistic* religions, or varieties of *theism*. Richard Swinburne, the former Nolloth Professor of the Christian Religion at Oxford University, has described theism as the claim that there is someone "without a body (i.e. a spirit) who is eternal, free, able to do anything, knows everything, is perfectly good, is the proper object of human worship and obedience, the creator and sustainer of the universe" (Swinburne, 1993, p. 1). In other words, theism is the claim that there is a God, that God exists. Focusing our inquiry on this claim, so central to Judaism, Christianity, and Islam, will allow us to organize our critical thinking on issues suggested by it. For example, does God exist? Can it be proven that there is a God? Or, can it be proven that there is no God? What does it mean to say that someone is "able to do anything"? Is it possible for there to be an *omnipotent* being? What is involved in someone who "knows everything"? If God is *omniscient*, does his knowledge extend to the future? And, if it does, is that compatible with human beings acting freely? If God is "the creator and sustainer of the universe," is he able to interfere with it? Are miracles possible, and might it be rational to think that miracles have occurred? Finally, if no proof can be found of God's existence, could it nevertheless be reasonable to believe in his existence? Is it always wrong to believe something without good evidence in its favor? How are faith and reason related?[2]

Arguments and Proving God's Existence

Since our first topic is the attempt to prove that God exists, the remainder of this chapter will discuss some key concepts that will prove helpful in pursuing this topic. Although our discussion will be framed in terms of proving the existence of God, the concepts and ideas we'll introduce here will also apply to the attempt to prove God's nonexistence, as well as the attempt to establish anything on any of the topics we will take up in the course of this book.

A proof of God's existence might be thought to give a really good reason to believe that God exists. I suggested above that we could distinguish a thesis from reasons for believing that thesis by construing the reasons as the *premisses* of an *argument* that has that thesis as a *conclusion*. Accordingly, we could start with the idea that a proof of God's existence is an argument that has the proposition that God exists as its conclusion, where an argument is simply a list of sentences or propositions, one of which is designated as the conclusion.

Of course, not just any argument that has *God exists* as its conclusion would be a good argument. For starters, we should want the conclusion to *follow from* the premises. It's not easy to say exactly what "follows from" amounts to. Fortunately, there is a relatively clear concept that we can employ instead, namely, that of an argument being *valid*, where that term is defined as follows:

(D1)   An argument is *valid* $=_{df}$ it is not possible for the premises of the argument to be true and the conclusion false.[3]

We can also introduce a term to describe an argument that is not valid, namely,

(D2)   An argument is *invalid* =$_{df}$ it is not valid.

An argument will be invalid just in case it fails to satisfy the definition of being valid, that is, just in case it *is* possible for its premises to be true and conclusion false. We can use the more precise term "valid" to give an account of the informal concept of a conclusion "following from" some premises as follows: a conclusion follows from a set of premises if and only if the argument with those premises and that conclusion is valid.

We can gain a better understanding of validity by considering some examples of arguments.

Example 1:

    (1)   Every human being is mortal.
    (2)   Socrates is a human being.
∴ (3)   Socrates is mortal. (1) (2)

The symbol "∴" in front of line (3) abbreviates the word "therefore." Thus, (3) is a conclusion, and the numbers in parentheses at the end of it indicate that it is a conclusion from the premises, lines (1) and (2). This argument is *valid*. It satisfies the definition of validity given in (D1) because it is not possible for its premises to be true and conclusion false. Here is another example:

Example 2:

    (1)   If you study hard, you will pass your philosophy course.
    (2)   You study hard.
∴ (3)   You will pass your philosophy course. (1) (2)

This argument has a different form, but it, too, is valid. There is no way the premises could be true but the conclusion false. If you think that you can imagine a scenario in which the conclusion is false but the premises are true, for example, a scenario in which you study hard but sleep through the tests and so you don't pass the course, that will invariably be a scenario in which at least one of the premises is false. In the example I just gave, the first premise would be false if you studied hard but didn't pass. There simply is no way things could go according to which the premises of this argument would be true and the conclusion would be false, but that is what would be required for this argument to fail to be valid.

Here is a related example:

Example 3:

    (1)   If you study hard, you will pass your philosophy course.
    (2)   You don't study hard.
∴   (3)   You won't pass your philosophy course. (1) (2)

This argument is *invalid*. There are many ways things could go according to which the premisses are true but the conclusion is false. Perhaps you don't study hard but pass the course on native ability. That's compatible with the truth of premiss (1), which only gives a sufficient condition for passing this course, leaving it open that there are other ways to pass. A sufficiently large bribe to the instructor might be one of those other ways.

If it wasn't obvious that Example 3 is invalid, there's a useful strategy, one we'll use repeatedly, for showing that an argument is invalid.

(**Strategy**)   **To show that an argument is invalid, find another argument of the same form with true premisses and a false conclusion.**

To apply this strategy we should notice that Example 3 has the following form:

    If p then q.
    Not-p.
∴   Not-q.

So we should look for another argument that has this form. If it *actually has* true premisses and a false conclusion, we know that it is *possible* for it to have true premisses and a false conclusion. In that case, it is invalid. But since the validity of an argument depends upon its form, any other argument of the same form is also invalid. Here is one:

Example 4:

    (1)   If it is warmer than 100 °F today, then it is warmer than –20 °F today.
    (2)   It's not warmer than 100 °F today.
∴   (3)   It's not warmer than –20 °F today.[4]

If we want a proof of God's existence, it would be useful to find a valid argument for the conclusion that God exists. But that's not all we would need, for a valid argument could nevertheless have a false conclusion. Consider:

Example 5:

      (1) If donkeys can fly, then donkeys have wings.
      (2) Donkeys can fly.
∴   (3) Donkeys have wings. (1) (2)

This argument is of the same form as Example 2, which we have seen to be valid; so this argument is valid, as well. But there is something egregiously wrong with it, because its conclusion is manifestly false. This does not show that there is a flaw in our concept of validity; after all, falsehoods have consequences, too, and we often draw conclusions from propositions without regard to whether they are true. But it shows that for an argument to be good, validity isn't the whole story. It's easy enough to see where the flaw lies, however: not only is the conclusion false, but the second premiss of the argument is false. So we should also recognize that a good argument has true premisses. The term for a valid argument with true premisses is "sound."

   (D3) An argument is *sound* $=_{df}$ it is valid and all its premisses are true.

As in the case of validity, we can also define the opposite of sound:

   (D4) An argument is *unsound* $=_{df}$ it is not sound.

A little bit of thought will show that it follows from (D1) and (D3) that a sound argument has a true conclusion. So if we want to prove that God exists, or if we want to prove anything else, it's tempting to think that what we need is a sound argument for that conclusion. Unfortunately, things aren't that simple. Consider:

Example 6:

      (1) Either nothing exists or God exists.
      (2) Something exists.
∴   (3) God exists.

This argument is sound, but it fails as a proof.[5] People to whom I have presented this argument usually agree that Example 6 is a bad proof, but they sometimes balk at agreeing that it's a sound argument. It clearly is valid: the first premiss says that at least one of two propositions is true; the second premiss adds that it isn't the first of them; so that leaves the second as the only option. Something exists, so (2) is true. Now I think that (1) is true, too, so I think that Example 6 is a sound argument that is a terrible proof.

Of course, I only think that (1) is true because I also think that God exists. Perhaps you don't share that view. Then consider this argument:

Example 7:

   (1)   Either nothing exists or God doesn't exist.
   (2)   Something exists.
∴ (3)   God doesn't exist.

Both Example 6 and Example 7 are valid (they're of the form logicians call *disjunctive syllogism*). They are also both terrible proofs. Now either God exists, or he does not. If God does exist, then Example 6 is a sound argument. If God doesn't exist, then Example 7 is a sound argument. Either way, there is a sound argument that is a terrible proof, and that is the point I was trying to make.

So if we want to find a proof of God's existence, we should look for a valid argument with true premisses. But what else should we insist on? Can we specify anything further about what the premisses should be like? It would be too strong to require that the premisses be accepted by *everyone*. As we'll see in the next chapter, Thomas Aquinas gives an argument for God's existence that takes as a premiss *Whatever begins to exist is caused to begin to exist by something already existing*. This premiss shouldn't be disallowed on the grounds that some people do not believe it. Some people have never even considered it and thus do not believe it; others who have considered it, but not carefully or with inadequate preparation, do not believe it. In any event, enough people believe so many obviously false propositions that it would set an impossibly high standard if arguments had to satisfy everyone.[6] Perhaps the best we can do is to say that for an argument to be useful as a proof, its premisses ought to seem to be true to nearly any reasonable, educated person who considers them carefully. Alternatively, a sound argument is good proof if it gives someone who understands it a reason to believe the conclusion that he or she would not have without understanding the argument. This remains less clear than is desirable, but perhaps we will be able to tell in particular cases whether an argument meets this standard. In any event, we should agree that whatever standards we set for arguments in favor of God's existence must also apply to arguments against God's existence and to the other arguments we will take up in later chapters.

One final point before we begin to look at some specific arguments for God's existence. You might think that there simply are no good proofs in philosophy, so we can tell in advance that there is no good argument for God's existence. But why should we think that there are no good proofs in philosophy? Surely there is no proof of that claim, because any such proof would be a good proof in philosophy; the existence of such a proof would refute its conclusion. So there seems to be no shortcut that avoids looking at the details of some attempted arguments for God's existence, which is what we will begin to do in the next chapter.

Notes

1 I follow Alonzo Church (1956), p. 2, in using the spelling "premiss" (rather than "premise") for a proposition included in a logical argument in support of its conclusion. This makes it easy to distinguish the plural from the legal term, "premises," which refers to a house or other building and its surrounding land.

2 I've just used some masculine pronouns to refer to God. I should emphasize that this is not because I think that God is male. Since God is, in Swinburne's phrase, "without a body." it follows that God has neither chromosomes nor physical sexual characteristics. So God is not male. For similar reasons, God is not female. It would make as much sense to use feminine pronouns as masculine, but that usage is not traditional. It would be a bad idea, however, to try to avoid the issue by using instead the ungendered pronoun "it"; for "it" is an impersonal pronoun, and God, as someone who knows and acts, is a person.

3 "$=_{df}$" is to be read *means by definition*. A more careful way to define validity proceeds in two steps. First, an *argument* is valid just in case it has a valid form. Second, an argument *form* is valid just in case it is not possible for an argument of that form to have true premises and a false conclusion. This more elaborate definition allows that an argument can have more than one form, it doesn't automatically count an argument with a conclusion that can't possibly be false as valid, and it makes explicit why we go on below to discuss argument forms. With apologies to purists, I'll continue using the simpler formulation in the text.

4 The conclusion (3) is false where I'm writing in balmy Rochester, New York.

5 This example is from Mavrodes (1970), p. 22.

6 According to an article in the *New York Times*, "Scientific Savvy? In U.S., Not Much" (August 30, 2005), 20 percent of Americans believe that the sun revolves around the earth. Many people are similarly misinformed about the age of the earth or the birthplace of President Barack Obama.

Suggested Reading

Stephen T. Davis, *God, Reason, and Theistic Proofs*, chapter 1, "What Is a Theistic Proof?" (Grand Rapids, MI.: Wm. B. Eerdmans, 1997).

Helen De Cruz, "The Enduring Appeal of Natural Theological Arguments," *Philosophy Compass* 9/2 (2014): 145–153.

George Mavrodes, *Belief in God* (New York: Random House, 1970).

Richard Swinburne, *Is There a God?*, chapter 1, "God" (Oxford and New York: Oxford University Press, 1996).

2

The Cosmological Argument for God's Existence

Insights from the Past

We said in the last chapter that we would organize our investigation of the philosophy of religion by focusing on a claim central to the major western theistic religions, Judaism, Christianity, and Islam, namely, that there is a God who is all-powerful, all-knowing, perfectly good, and who is the creator and sustainer of the universe. We will begin by asking whether this claim can be shown to be true. Later we'll ask whether it can be shown to be false. Finally, we'll take a closer look at the properties attributed to God by theism.

One respect in which philosophy differs from many other disciplines is the interest it takes in its figures of the past. While many of Newton's physical theories have been superseded by the theories of relativity and quantum mechanics, and no physician today would consult, say, the work of Dr Benjamin Rush (one of the signers of the Declaration of Independence) for advice about bloodletting, philosophers look to the work of earlier figures for insight and inspiration. Not only have many of the topics that historical philosophers discussed remained of real interest, but the problems they identified and the solutions they advanced often provide a good starting place for working through the issues ourselves. This phenomenon is perhaps nowhere more pervasive than in philosophy of religion, where the great philosophers and theologians of late antiquity and the Middle Ages explicitly aimed at providing a philosophical account of topics that we recognize as central to philosophy of religion. Thus, such classical theists as Augustine of Hippo (354–430 CE), Anselm of Canterbury (1033–1109), and Thomas Aquinas (1225–1274) in the Christian tradition; Moses Maimonides (1135–1204) in the Jewish tradition; and

The Philosophy of Religion, First Edition. Edward R. Wierenga.
© 2016 Edward R. Wierenga. Published 2016 by John Wiley & Sons, Ltd.

Ibn Sīnā, or Avicenna, to use his Latinized name, (c. 980–1037) in the Islamic tradition, wrote with sophistication on the nature of God and on arguments for his existence. Subsequent philosophers of the period known as Modern Philosophy, whether they intended to support or refute theism, took a real interest in philosophical analysis of topics in religion and did much to advance the discussion. I'll mention just three, whom we'll have occasion to cite later: the French rationalist René Descartes (1596–1650), the Scottish empiricist David Hume (1711–1776), and the German philosopher Immanuel Kant (1724–1804). Hume's posthumously published *Dialogues Concerning Natural Religion* (Hume, 1947 [1779]), in particular, set the agenda for much of philosophy of religion for the following two centuries. Our approach to issues in the philosophy of religion will be to begin by looking at what earlier philosophers said. Then we'll use that as a springboard for our own attempt to think through the issues.

Arguments for God's Existence

There are many ways people have attempted to argue for God's existence. Some arguments appeal to religious experience, perhaps an intense mystical experience or an overwhelming response to a scene of beauty or an act of kindness. Some philosophers have given a "moral argument," claiming that there could be no moral laws without a supreme law-giver. But we will focus on examples of the big three arguments, the *cosmological*, the *ontological*, and the *teleological*, to use the terms that Kant invented. Cosmological arguments take the general form of appealing to the existence of the cosmos, or the world, or things existing in the world, and arguing that these things would exist only if there was a creator or a first cause. The ontological argument holds that from the very idea or concept of God as a perfect being or as that than which nothing greater can be conceived, in Anselm's famous phrase, it simply follows directly that God exists. Teleological arguments, or arguments from design, hold that the evident patterns of design in the universe provide convincing evidence of God's existence.

A Cosmological Argument: Aquinas' Third Way

In his *Summa Theologiae* (Ia, 2, 3) Thomas Aquinas (1948 [1485]) said that there are five ways of proving God's existence. If a cosmological argument for God's existence is one that reasons from a premiss that there is something existing now to the conclusion that there is a God, then several of Aquinas' "Five Ways" are cosmological arguments. One way begins from the premiss that there are things that are changing or in motion to deduce that there is an unmoved First Mover. Another begins with the premiss that there are events which are caused by other events to argue for the conclusion that there is a First Cause. We'll take a closer look at Aquinas' Third Way, which attempts to establish that there is a being of a very special sort, one that is necessary or that exists necessarily. Let's start by looking at what Aquinas says:

> The third way is taken from possibility and necessity, and runs thus. We find in nature things that are possible to be and not to be, since they are found to be generated, and to be corrupted, and consequently, it is possible for them to be and not to be. But it impossible for these always to exist, for that which can not-be at some time is not. Therefore, if everything can not-be, then at one time there was nothing in existence. Now if this were true, even now there would be nothing in existence, because that which does not exist begins to exist only through something already existing. Therefore, if at one time nothing was in existence, it would have been impossible for anything to have begun to exist; and thus even now nothing would be in existence – which is absurd. Therefore, not all beings are merely possible, but there must exist something the existence of which is necessary. But every necessary being either has its necessity caused by another, or not. Now it is impossible to go to infinity in necessary things which have their necessity caused by another, as has been already proved in regard to efficient causes. Therefore we cannot but admit the existence of some being having of itself its own necessity, and not receiving it from another, but rather causing in others their necessity. This all men speak of as God. (Aquinas, 1948 [1485], *Summa Theologiae*, Ia, 2, 3)

Aquinas begins his argument by holding that "we find in nature things that are possible to be and not to be, since they are found to be generated, and to be corrupted, and consequently, it is possible for them to be and not to be." Let's call these things that are "possible to be and not to be" *contingent beings*. We'll need to look more closely below at the concepts of possibility and necessity. For now let's simply note that the second phrase in Aquinas' sentence begins with the word "since." That's often a clue that what comes next is a reason for what was just asserted. In this case, Aquinas' reason for holding that there are some contingent beings is that there are things that are generated and corrupted. He means, I believe, that we are aware of things that come into existence and of things that go out of existence. Anything that comes into existence really does exist and so it is such that it is possible that it exists, and, of course, before such a thing begins to exist it does not exist, and so it is possible that it not exist. Similarly, things that go out of existence really do exist before they go out of existence, and they fail to exist later; they also possibly exist and possibly do not exist.

What sort of things are these? Well, you and I came into existence, so we possibly exist and possibly do not exist. There is no doubt about whether we do exist, but the fact that we came into existence shows that there are ways things could go according to which we exist and ways they could go according to which we do not exist. The earth and everything on it came into existence, so all these things are contingent, too. And some things that used to exist no longer do – they were "corrupted" – like the last dodo in the late 17th century. So that gives us another example of a contingent being. Let's take the first premiss of Aquinas's argument, then, as the claim

(1)   There are some contingent beings,

understanding it and Aquinas's reason in support of it along the lines we have just been discussing.

Aquinas next adds that anything that "can not-be at some time is not." He thus endorses the claim that

(2)   For every contingent being, there is a time when it does not exist.

What Aquinas says next is a little puzzling, however. He seems to deduce that "if everything can not-be, then at one time there was nothing in existence." But how does this follow? Presumably Aquinas makes an inference from (2), deducing that

(3)   There is a time at which every contingent being does not exist.

From that he derives his claim that

(4)   If all beings are contingent, then at one time nothing existed.

He then adds, "Now if this were true [that at one time nothing existed], even now there would be nothing in existence, because that which does not exist begins to exist only through something already existing. Therefore, if at one time nothing was in existence, it would have been impossible for anything to have begun to exist; and thus even now nothing would be in existence – which is absurd." In this passage he asserts an additional premiss (following the word "because" – another hint that an author is giving a reason):

> (5)   Whatever begins to exist is caused to begin to exist by something already existing.

He then deduces

> (6)   If at one time nothing existed, nothing exists now,

and

> (7)   If all beings are contingent, nothing exists now.

Aquinas thinks that is absurd to hold that nothing exists now, and in fact the first premiss of his argument asserts that some contingent beings exist (now). So he concludes that

> (8)   Not all beings are contingent.

And from this he deduces that

> (9)   There is at least one necessary being.

It is clear how the rest of the argument is supposed to go, even if some of the ideas are not entirely clear:

> (10)   Every necessary being either has its necessity caused by another, or it has its necessity of itself.
> (11)   There cannot be an infinite series of necessary beings each having its necessity caused by another.

So,

> (12)   There is a necessary being having of itself its own necessity (and this is God).

Putting these various claims together, we can formulate Aquinas' Third Way as follows:

> (1)   There are some contingent beings. (premiss)
> (2)   For every contingent being, there is a time when it does not exist. (premiss)
> ∴   (3)   There is a time at which every contingent being does not exist. (2)

∴　(4)　If all beings are contingent, then at one time nothing existed. (3)

　　(5)　Whatever begins to exist is caused to begin to exist by something already existing. (premiss)

∴　(6)　If at one time nothing existed, nothing exists now. (5)

∴　(7)　If all beings are contingent, nothing exists now. (4) (6)

∴　(8)　Not all beings are contingent. (1) (7)

∴　(9)　There is at least one necessary being. (8)

　(10)　Every necessary being either has its necessity caused by another, or it has its necessity of itself. (premiss)

　(11)　There cannot be an infinite series of necessary beings each having its necessity caused by another. (premiss)

∴　(12)　There is a necessary being having of itself its own necessity (and this is God). (9) (10) (11)

To evaluate this argument we will have two sorts of questions to consider: do we have reason to think that the various propositions labeled as premisses are true?, and do the propositions that are deduced from those premisses really follow from them, that is, are the inferences in the argument *valid*? Before we can make progress on this project, however, we should try to make sure that we understand some of the claims Aquinas makes. Since the concepts of possibility and necessity figure so prominently in the argument, we will begin by examining those concepts.

Possibility and Necessity: A Look at 'Modal' Concepts

Aquinas begins with the idea of a thing that is "possible to be" and also "possible not to-be." We can think of this as something that possibly exists and that possibly doesn't exist. But we have to be careful about how to understand that. When Aquinas talks about things that possibly exist and that possibly do not exist, he's not talking about things whose existence is uncertain. He doesn't mean to be talking about things like the Abominable Snowman or the Loch Ness Monster, whose existence is disputed. Someone who was uncertain about whether the Loch Ness Monster exists might say that it is possible that it exists and possible that it doesn't exist, intending thereby to express *epistemic* possibility. This means, roughly, that the existence of the Loch Ness Monster and its nonexistence are each compatible with what the person knows, or, perhaps, with what that person's evidence supports. I interpret Aquinas instead as being concerned with *metaphysical* possibility. One reason for thinking this is that Aquinas cites, as examples of the kinds of things he has in mind, things for which there is no question as to whether they exist or fail to exist – these are things we "find in nature." A second reason is that his appeal to things that are generated or are corrupted – that come into existence or that go out of existence – can naturally, as we saw above, be understood as specifying *a way things can go*. If a thing begins to exist, then there is a way things could go according to which it *does not* exist – the way things were before it began to exist – and there is a way things could go according to which it *does* exist – the way things went in which it does exist. Such ways things could go are *possibilities*.

Here are some principles to make this idea a little more formal:

(a) It is possible that a thing *x* exists just in case there is a way things could go according to which, if they went that way, *x* would exist.

(b) It is possible that a thing *x* does not exist just in case there is a way things could go according to which, if they went that way, *x* would not exist.

These principles have to do with possible *existence*, which is the topic Aquinas begins with. But they can be adapted to apply to metaphysical possibility more generally or, as we'll state it, to possible *truth*:

(c) It is possible that a proposition *p* is true (or *p* is possibly true) just in case there is a way things could go according to which, if they went that way, *p* would be true.

(d) It is possible that a proposition *p* is false (or *p* is possibly false) just in case there is a way things could go according to which, if they went that way, *p* would be false.

We have already employed this concept of possibility when, in the last chapter, we defined a valid argument as one in which it is not possible for the premises of the argument to be true and the conclusion false. If an argument is valid, there is no way things could go according to which the premises of the argument would be true but the conclusion false.

Propositions that are possibly true report ways things could be. Every proposition that is in fact true is thereby possibly true, because the way things are is a way they can be. But some propositions that are false could have been true instead. *The sun has more than 10 planets orbiting it* is false, but it could have been true. *The Chicago Cubs will win the World Series in my lifetime* is false (or so I think), but even it could have been true. In fact, many completely preposterous propositions are possibly true. But some propositions could not have been true – there is no way things could go according to which such propositions as *some triangles have four sides* or *there is a married bachelor* are true. Such propositions are *impossible*. Other propositions would be true no matter how things go. *All triangles have three sides, no bachelor is married*, and *if p is true and q is true then the conjunction of p & q is true* are all propositions that *have* to be true. They are necessarily true. We can add to our list of principles:

(e) It is necessary that a proposition *p* is true (or *p* is necessarily true) just in case every way things could go is a way according to which *p* would be true.

(f) It is impossible that a proposition *p* is true (or *p* is impossible) just in case there is no way things could go according to which, if they went that way, *p* would be true.

It is a consequence of (c) and (e) that if a proposition is necessary then it is possible, because a proposition that is true in *every* way things could go is true in *some* way things could go.[1]

We defined a *possible being* in principle (a) above as a being for which there is a way things could go according to which it would exist. By parallel reasoning, we could explain a necessary being as follows:

(g) It is necessary that a thing *x* exists just in case every way things could go is a way according to which *x* would exist.

Back to the Third Way

Our digression into modal matters puts us in a position to appreciate an inference Aquinas makes in the Third Way. From

(8) Not all beings are contingent

he deduces that

(9) There is at least one necessary being.

If (8) is true, there is at least one being that is non-contingent. A contingent being is one such that (a) it is possible that it exists and also (b) possible that it does not exist. A being that is not contingent would therefore fail to satisfy one of the other of these two conditions (or both – but that isn't possible). Either it is *not* possible that it exists or *not* possible that it does not exist. But there couldn't be a being of the first sort, a being that doesn't possibly exist. So if there is something that is not a contingent being, it is a being such that it is *not possible that it not exist*. But that is just to say that it exists no matter how things go; in other words, it is a necessary being. So our interpretation of contingent, possible, and necessary beings has the virtue of vindicating a crucial inference in the argument, namely, the step from (8) to (9).

A Question Remains

Unfortunately, what we have said so far does not help us understand another key part of the argument. Aquinas distinguishes between necessary beings that have their necessity "caused by another" and necessary beings that have their necessity of themselves. But what could it mean for a necessary being to have its necessity caused by another? If a being really is necessary, then, as we have understood this idea, such a being would exist no matter how things go. In that case, however, it is hard to see how there is anything a second being could do that would make the first being necessary, because whatever the second being did or failed to do, the first being would still exist. If it is necessary, it exists no matter what. Perhaps this is not a serious problem for the argument, however. If there couldn't be any necessary beings having their necessity caused by another, Aquinas' claim that

> (10)   Every necessary being either has its necessity caused by another, or it has its necessity of itself

might still be true – if every necessary being has its necessity of itself, then, trivially, it either has it of itself or caused by another. And if there couldn't be *any* necessary beings having their necessity caused by another, *a fortiori*, there couldn't be *an infinite series* of them. In that case

> (11)   There cannot be an infinite series of necessary beings each having its necessity caused by another

would be true, and it would still follow from (9), (10), and (11) that

> (12)   There is a necessary being having of itself its own necessity.[2]

A More Substantial Objection

If the conclusion of the argument is simply that there is a necessary being, even with the additional stipulation that it has its necessity of itself, why does Aquinas think that this is what everyone calls *God*? Or, instead of trying to answer this historical question, let us ask why we should think that a necessary being is God. Notice first that the argument does not purport to show that there is a unique or only one necessary being – what follows from *not all beings are contingent* is that *at least one being is necessary*, which is compatible with there being many necessary beings. And, in fact, if a necessary being is one that exists in every set of circumstances – exists no matter which way things go – then there are indeed many such beings. The proposition that *there are human beings* is true in many of the ways things could go, and it is false in all the rest of the ways things could go. So, no matter what things are like, that proposition is either true or false, and in either case it would exist. Similarly, the property of *being a human being* is had or instantiated by human beings just in case there are human beings, and it is not instantiated, otherwise. However things go, therefore, it is either instantiated or not, and in either case it would exist. Finally, such mathematical objects as natural numbers exist necessarily, for no matter how things go, the number 12 is larger than the number five, and it is divisible by four. And it couldn't be larger than another number or divisible by another number without existing itself. Such abstract objects as propositions, properties, or numbers, while they may exist necessarily, do not have some of the other impressive properties a divine being should have – they are not omnipotent or omniscient or able to do things, for example. For all we have seen so far, Aquinas' Third Way might be a sound argument, but it does not seem to be an argument for the existence of God.[3]

Some Compelling Objections

We should look a little more closely at the initial steps in the argument. Recall that the second premiss is

(2)   For every contingent being, there is a time when it does not exist.

Should we accept this premiss? It is not obviously or self-evidently true. As we have seen, a contingent being is a being that does not have to exist – things could go or could have gone in a way such that it doesn't exist. But does it follow that for any such being there is a time when in fact it does not exist? Couldn't a contingent being be everlasting, existing at every time, while nevertheless being such that it might not have existed? At any rate, I see nothing incoherent in the idea of a contingent being that never fails to exist. Someone who shares this view might well find (2) dubious.

Having said this, I should acknowledge that I think that (2) is true. I think it is true because I think that God created contingent beings and before he did none of them existed. So I think it is true that for every contingent being there is a time at which it does not exist, namely any time before God created. Of course, it would be wildly inappropriate in the present context to defend (2) by appealing to God's creative activity. If the existence of God is what is to be shown, it would not be a good way to attempt to do this by appealing to the prior assumption that he is the Creator. We should, accordingly, concede at a minimum that premiss (2) stands in need of additional support and that, in any event, for many people it will not seem compelling.

Finally, there is a decisive objection to the *validity* of the argument. Aquinas appears to infer from (2) that

(3)   There is a time at which every contingent being does not exist.

This inference is invalid. We saw in the last chapter that a useful strategy to show that an argument is invalid is to find another argument of the same form with true premisses and a false conclusion. Given that the validity of an argument depends upon its logical form, this is a way of showing how it is possible for an argument to have true premisses and a false conclusion by finding an instance in which it does. Here is such a case:

(2')   For every road, there is a destination to which that road leads.
∴ (3')   There is a destination to which every road leads. (2')[4]

Presumably every road goes somewhere, if only to a dead-end, but it is not true that there is some place to which every road goes. Logicians call such expression as "for every" and "there is" *quantifiers*. What this example shows is that the order of quantifiers matters; they cannot always be switched in a sentence and preserve truth.

I think that this version of the cosmological argument is unsuccessful. There's a reason, in the first place, to question whether it even is an argument for *God's* existence; it has at least one disputable premiss, (2); and a crucial inference, that of (3) from (2) is invalid. In the next chapter we will look at another attempt to prove that God exists.

Notes

1   The branch of logic that investigates the logical properties of possibility and necessity is called *modal logic*. For some additional details about these ideas and about understanding them by reference to possible worlds, see the discussion of A Modal Interlude: Possible Worlds in Chapter 5.

2   Alternatively, given the triviality of these extra steps, the argument could simply end with (9). Interestingly, that is how Kant characterized the cosmological argument: "If we admit something as existing, no matter what this something may be, we must also admit that there is something which exists *necessarily*. For the contingent exists only under the condition of some other contingent existence as its cause and from this again we must infer yet another cause, until we are brought to a cause which is not contingent, and which is therefore unconditionally necessary. This is the argument upon which reason bases its advance to the primordial being" (Kant, 1929, *Critique of Pure Reason*, book II, chapter 3, section 3).

3   Compare Kant's claim, "...it by no means follows that the concept of a limited being which does not have the highest reality is for that reason incompatible with absolute necessity," and later, "we are entirely free to hold that any limited beings whatsoever, notwithstanding their being limited, may also be unconditionally necessary...." Kant's conclusion, however, is stronger than the one I have been arguing for, since he holds that "the argument has failed to give us the least concept of the properties of a necessary being, and indeed is utterly ineffective" (Kant, 1929, *Critique of Pure Reason*, book II, chapter 3, section 3).

4   This example is from Kenny in *The Five Ways* (1980), p. 56.

Suggested Reading

Thomas Aquinas, *Summa Theologiae*, in *Introduction to St. Thomas Aquinas*, ed., Anton Pegis (New York: Modern Library, 1948) (Ia, q. 1–2).

Anthony Kenny, *The Five Ways: Aquinas' Proofs of God's Existence*, chapter 4 (London: Routledge and Kegan Paul, 1969; reprinted South Bend, IN: University of Notre Dame Press, 1980).

Alvin Plantinga, *God, Freedom, and Evil* (New York: Harper and Row, 1974; reprinted Grand Rapids, MI: Wm. B. Eerdmans, 1977), pp. 75–80.

3

The Ontological Argument

One of the most puzzling and intriguing arguments for God's existence was first formulated in the 11th century by Anselm of Canterbury, the abbot of a monastery in Normandy and later Archbishop of Canterbury. Anselm's ontological argument has fascinated philosophers ever since it was first propounded. In fact, from the very beginning Anselm's manuscript was circulated with a set of objections by one of his contemporaries, a monk named Gaunilo, together with Anselm's replies. A remarkable number of subsequent philosophers have had something to say about the argument. Thomas Aquinas, for example, offered an objection to it, and René Descartes gave his own version, although one that was very much in the spirit of Anselm. This pattern of objection, reply, a new version, and a new objection continued until Immanuel Kant claimed to refute all versions, and many philosophers believed him. In 1960, however, the world of professional philosophers was shocked when Norman Malcolm published a paper defending a version of the argument in a highly respected academic journal (Malcolm, 1960). Malcolm's essay ushered in a new era of interest in the argument, one in which philosophers attempted to put recent developments in logic and in other areas of philosophy to use in understanding the argument.[1]

Anselm's Statement of the Argument

Anselm's argument is found in chapter 2 of his work *Proslogion*, embedded in a prayer:

> Well then, Lord, You who give understanding to faith, grant me that I may understand, as much as You see fit, that You exist as we believe You to exist,

The Philosophy of Religion, First Edition. Edward R. Wierenga.
© 2016 Edward R. Wierenga. Published 2016 by John Wiley & Sons, Ltd.

and that You are what we believe You to be. Now we believe that You are something than which nothing greater can be thought. Or can it be that a thing of such a nature does not exist, since "The fool has said in his heart, 'There is no God'" (Psalm 13:1, 52:1)? But surely, when this same Fool hears what I am speaking about, namely, "something-than-which-nothing-greater-can-be-thought," he understands what he hears, and what he understands is in his mind, even if he does not understand that it actually exists. For it is one thing for an object to exist in the mind, and another to understand that an object actually exists. Thus, when a painter plans beforehand what he is going to execute, he has [the picture] in his understanding, but he does not yet think that it actually exists, because he has not yet executed it. However, when he has actually painted it, then he both has it in his mind and understands that it exists because he has now made it. Even the Fool, then, is forced to agree that something-than-which-nothing-greater-can-be-thought exists in the mind, since he understands this when he hears it, and whatever is understood is in the mind. And surely that-than-which-a-greater-cannot-be-thought cannot exist in the mind alone. For if it exists solely in the mind, it can be thought to exist in reality also, which is greater. If then that-than-which-a greater-cannot-be-thought exists in the mind alone, this same that-than-which-a-greater-*cannot*-be-thought is that-than-which-a-greater-*can*-be-thought. But this is obviously impossible. Therefore there is absolutely no doubt that something-than-which-a-greater-cannot-be-thought exists both in the mind and in reality. (Anselm of Canterbury, 1998, pp. 87–88)

Preliminaries

The prayer with which Anselm begins asks God to give him understanding of what he believes by faith. In fact the phrase *fides quaerens intellectum*, "faith seeking understanding," was Anselm's original title for the work and serves as its motto. Anselm thus begins with faith in God, but he aims at deepening his understanding of what he already believes by showing that it follows from the very nature of God that he exists. The first preliminary point we need to note, then, is that Anselm offers a definition or an account of that nature: God is that "than-which-nothing-greater-can-be-thought." In later chapters of the *Proslogion* Anselm expands on what he means by greatness, giving the formula that "God is whatever it is better to be than not" and then concluding that this includes "existing through Himself alone," making other things from nothing, being just, being happy, and being perceptive, omnipotent, and merciful, among other things.

A second preliminary point is that Anselm introduces a distinction between existing in the mind or the understanding and existing in reality. We can think of this as a distinction between existing in thought and really existing. In Anselm's example, a painting that a painter plans out in advance and then later executes exists initially only in thought and then later, after the painter has done the work, exists in reality as well.

Finally, part of Anselm's genius, I think, was his development of the argument as a *reductio ad absurdum*.[2] This is a form of argument, literally "reduction to absurdity," that proceeds by assuming the denial of what is to be shown, (optionally, but typically) adding some additional premisses, and then deducing a contradiction. If an assumption and some premisses together entail a contradiction, then, if the premisses are true, it follows that the assumption is the culprit. So if an initial assumption made for the sake of argument is shown in this way to be false, its denial, the proposition that was to be demonstrated, is true.

A Statement of the Argument

I said above that Anselm's argument was embedded in the quoted passage, but it is open to interpretation exactly where the argument occurs and exactly what its premisses are.[3] I think that the clause "surely that than which a greater cannot be thought cannot exist only in the understanding" states the conclusion of the argument and that the following sentences, beginning with the word "for," give the reasons or premisses in support of that conclusion. If this is right, we can formulate the argument as follows, where "B" is a name whose reference is fixed by the description "the being than which a greater cannot be conceived":[4]

(1)   B does not exist. (assumption for *reductio ad absurdum*)
(2)   For all x, if x does not exist, then it is conceivable that there is something greater than x. (premiss)
∴ (3)   If B does not exist, then it is conceivable that there is a being greater than B. (2), universal instantiation
∴ (4)   It is conceivable that there is something greater than B. (1) (3)
(5)   It is not conceivable that there is something greater than B. (premiss)
∴ (6)   B exists. (1)–(5), *reductio ad absurdum*

Some initial comments: Anselm does not explicitly state premiss (2). He merely says that if a thing "exists only in the understanding, it can be thought to exist in reality as well, which is greater." He thus clearly intends to appeal to some general principle connecting greatness and existence, and (2) seems to be an obvious and plausible candidate. Anselm also does not explicitly assert (5), but he does say about the statement I have given as line (4) that it is "obviously impossible," which suggests that he means, at a minimum, to assert the denial of (4), which is what (5) is.

One of the intriguing features of the argument is that it purports to demonstrate God's existence *a priori*, that is, without appeal to any evidence or experience of the world. In this respect it differs from the cosmological argument, which has the premiss that there are some contingent beings, a claim one could only reasonably believe on the basis of evidence or experience. And the argument we will consider in the next chapter requires evidence of the patterns of design the universe exhibits. In contrast, if the ontological argument succeeds, you could prove God's existence in your armchair, just by thinking about it.

It might seem astounding that one could prove God's existence in this way, but the argument has only two premisses, both of which seem credible. Premiss (2) says that if a thing doesn't exist, then it is conceivable that there be something greater. Anselm's thought seems to be that if a thing doesn't exist, then there is a way that that very thing could be improved, namely, by existing. This is perhaps a slightly stronger claim than he really needs – it would be enough if something or other could be conceived to be greater. But even Anselm's version seems plausible. Pick your favorite nonexistent being, say, Superman. Despite the many impressive attributes of the Man of Steel, *being more powerful than a locomotive*, among others, wouldn't Superman be even greater if, in addition to having superpowers, he also existed? Isn't existence one of those properties it is better to have than not? If so, it is a great-making property, one that contributes to a thing's greatness. The other premiss, (5), says that it is not conceivable that there be a being greater than B, who is, after all, a being than which it is not conceivable that there be a greater. This premiss even seems tautological. So the argument apparently deduces that God exists from a pair of plausible premisses.

Gaunilo's Objection

Nevertheless, as we noted, the argument has had its detractors. One of the most famous is the first recorded one, Anselm's fellow monk, Gaunilo of Marmoutiers. Gaunilo's "*Pro insipiente* (On Behalf of the Fool)"[5] raised a number of objections, the most well-known of which appeals to the greatest island. He writes

...they say that there is in the ocean somewhere an island which, because of the difficulty (or rather the impossibility) of finding that which does not exist, some have called the "Lost Island". And the story goes that it is blessed with all manner of priceless riches and delights in abundance, much more even than the Happy Isles, and, having no owner or inhabitant, it is superior everywhere in abundance of riches to all those other lands that men inhabit. Now, if anyone tell me that it is like this, I shall easily understand what is said, since nothing is difficult about it. But if he should then go on to say, as though it were a logical consequence of this: You cannot any more doubt that this island that is more excellent than all other lands truly exists somewhere in reality than you can doubt that it is in your mind; and since it is more excellent to exist not only in the mind alone but also in reality, therefore it must needs be that it exists. For if it did not exist, any other land existing in reality would be more excellent than it, and so this island, already conceived by you to be more excellent than others, will not be more excellent. If, I say, someone wishes thus to persuade me that this island really exists beyond all doubt, I should either think that he was joking, or I should find it hard to decide which of us I ought to judge the bigger fool – I, if I agreed with him, or he, if he thought that he had proved the existence of this island with any certainty, unless he had first convinced me that its very excellence exists in my mind precisely as a thing existing truly and indubitably and not just as something unreal or doubtfully real. (*Pro Insipiente* (*On Behalf of the Fool*), chapter 6; in Anselm of Canterbury (1998) *The Major Works*)

Gaunilo clearly thinks that the argument fails, but he is less clear about what the flaw really is. Since he doesn't apply his example to identify a false or dubious premiss, I think he is most plausibly interpreted as objecting to the validity of the argument;[6] in particular, he seems to be giving a recipe for constructing another argument of the same form as Anselm's but with true premisses and a false conclusion. We could thus take his objection as follows:

(Gaunilo)   Replacing the name "B" in Anselm's argument (above)[7] with the description "the greatest island" (an island superior to all other lands) creates an argument of the same form as Anselm's with true premisses and a false conclusion. Therefore, Anselm's argument is invalid.

Anselm's Reply

Anselm's reply to this objection seems to involve denying that the resulting argument really is of the same form as Anselm's. First, Anselm says, "I truly promise that if anyone should discover for me something existing either in reality or in the mind alone – except 'that-than-which-a-greater-cannot-be-thought' – to which the logic of my argument would apply, then I shall find that Lost Island and give it, never more to be lost, to that person." So Anselm thinks that his argument is somehow different from any such parody. Exactly why he thinks that the argument Gaunilo constructs is of a different form is suggested by a distinction Anselm goes on to draw. He says to Gaunilo that "you often reiterate that I say that that which is greater than everything exists in the mind, and that if it is in the mind, it exists also in reality, for otherwise that which is greater than everything would not be that which is greater than everything, However, nowhere in all that I have said will you find such an argument, for 'that which is greater than everything' and 'that-than-which-a-greater-cannot-be-thought' are not equivalent for the purpose of proving the real existence of the thing spoken of." Anselm thus claims that being the *greatest* is not the same as being the *greatest conceivable*.

No doubt Anselm is correct that there is a difference between the greatest something-or-other and the greatest conceivable. The greatest is greater than all others, which need not mean as great as can be or the greatest conceivable. For many categories of things, if there is a greatest, say, the greatest folk-rock singer or the greatest professional basketball player, there are ways in which those things could be improved – the former could have a slightly less gravelly voice, for example, and the latter could have scored more points per minute played. Gaunilo does indeed describe his Lost Island as "superior ... to all those other lands," without claiming that it is the greatest conceivable island, so perhaps his argument is not of the same form as Anselm's.

The Objection Revised

Nevertheless, it is easy enough to repair Gaunilo's objection to take account of Anselm's point – simply use instead the example of the greatest conceivable island. (This move is obvious enough that it probably occurred to Gaunilo, but we don't know what he thought about it.) Here is the revised objection:

(Gaunilo 2)   Replacing the name "B" in Anselm's argument (above) with the description "the greatest conceivable island" creates an argument of the same form as Anselm's with true premises and a false conclusion. Therefore, Anselm's argument is invalid.

This modest revision seems to avoid Anselm's claim that the resulting argument is not of the same form as Anselm's, and the two analogous premisses seem true. Moreover, the conclusion of the resulting argument,

    (6G)   The greatest conceivable island exists.

is obviously false.[8] As impressive as many of our actual islands are, none of them is so great that it is inconceivable that it be improved. So it looks like Gaunilo is correct in his claim that Anselm's is invalid.

We still haven't seen which particular inference in the argument is invalid, however, but the inference from (2) to (3) is certainly suspect:

        (2)   For all x, if x does not exist, then it is conceivable that there is something greater than x. (premiss)
$\therefore$ (3)   If B does not exist, then it is conceivable that there is a being greater than B. (2), universal instantiation

(2) is a general claim, a claim that is supposed to apply to everything. The inference to (3), an application of the rule of universal instantiation, applies that general claim to the particular thing B. Now universal instantiation is a valid rule of inference – any claim true of everything is true of any particular thing you pick. But it is only a valid form of inference when the general claim is applied to a particular thing that *exists*. If we apply a general or universal truth to a thing that doesn't exist, we could move from a truth to a falsehood. For example, it seems to be true that

    (2*)   For all x, if x is a boy, then x is at some spatio-temporal distance from here now.

Pick any boy, and he will be at some spatio-temporal distance from where you are right now, maybe nearby, maybe across the ocean, or maybe even far away and long ago. But it would be a mistake to infer from (2*) that:

    (3*)   If Harry Potter is a boy, then Harry Potter is at some spatio-temporal distance from here now. (2*), universal instantiation

Harry Potter is a boy, all right, but he is a fictional boy and is in no direction from where you are now. Similarly, since the greatest conceivable island does not exist, it is illegitimate to apply just any general truth to it, in particular, not the general truth, (2), that if it does not exist then it is conceivable that there is something greater than it. Finally, Anselm's own application of

(2) to B presupposes that B actually exists – if B does not exist, then it is a mistake to think that every universal truth applies to it. In other words, (3) follows from (2) only on the assumption that B exists. But this is precisely what the argument is intended to establish. It is not legitimate to assume that B exists in the process of attempting to prove it.

How to Talk about God without Presupposing that He Exists

Recent work by Lynne Baker and Gareth Matthews (Baker and Matthews, 2010) suggests a way of avoiding this objection. Central to their view is the idea that we can talk about things or persons without presupposing that they exist. That will allow a way for Anselm and his atheist opponent to discuss the being than which a greater cannot be conceived without assuming that such a being really exists. The second step in their proposal is to develop a way in which such beings could be compared with respect to greatness, again without assuming that they exist. Putting these two parts of the view together will allow us to give an alternate argument for

(4) It is conceivable that there is something greater than B.

that does not require a questionable use of universal instantiation.

Baker and Matthews first point out that we can talk about things whether they exist or not. In fact, people can talk about the same thing without agreeing about whether it exists. For example, people can talk about the Loch Ness Monster even if they don't all think that it exists. If they discuss its approximate length or the dates on which it has allegedly been sighted, they are talking about the same thing. Baker and Matthews call things that we can think about and discuss "objects of thought." They go on to draw a distinction, like Anselm's, between existing in reality and existing in the understanding. If the Loch Ness Monster really exists, then it is an object of thought that exists in reality; if it doesn't exist, it is an object of thought that exists in the understanding alone. Names that we introduce to talk about things can similarly vary in their reference. Thus, "Johnny Appleseed" or "Harry Potter" refer either to objects of thought that exist only in the understanding or to ones that exist in reality. As it turns out, the former refers to an actual person, John Chapman, while the latter refers to a *mere* object of thought.[9] People can use these names, however, to communicate with each other even if, say, some of them think that Johnny Appleseed is mythical or that Harry Potter is real.

Corresponding to the two modes of existence, according to Baker and Matthews, are two ways of possessing a property. An object of thought can have a property *in thought* or it can have it *in reality*. An object of thought has a property in thought if someone thinks of it as having that property, whereas an object of thought has a property in reality if, as one would expect, it really has it. For example, Harry Potter has-in-thought such properties as *having been born on July 31*, *having been orphaned*, and *being a wizard*, etc. But perhaps he has-in-reality the property of *having his name on the cover of millions of books*. An interesting feature of those objects of thought that exist only in the understanding is that they have-in-thought an incomplete set of properties. Harry Potter has-in-thought the properties listed above and many more, but he lacks-in-thought properties specifying his time of birth, his weight at birth, his blood type, and his body-mass index at age ten. By contrast, objects of thought that exist in reality have-in-reality a full set of properties: for any property P they either have it or they have *not-P*, the complement of P.

How to Be Greater than a Nonexistent Object

Baker and Matthews exploit the difference between having properties in reality versus having them in thought (and the fact that a thing that exists only in thought has-in-thought only a limited set of properties) to introduce a technical concept and then to give a sufficient condition for something being greater than a mere object of thought. The technical concept is the relation of *being an otherwise exact same thing as*, and it is defined as:

(OES)   If x exists merely in thought, then any y that exists in thought and in reality and has-in-reality all the properties that x has-in-thought is *an otherwise exact same thing as x*.

So if any real boy has the properties Harry Potter has-in-thought, for example, the properties in the set {*having been born on July 31*, *having been orphaned*, *being a wizard*, etc.}, then that real boy is an otherwise exact same thing as Harry Potter. The real boy will have these properties in reality, and he will have many more properties, as well.

Next, by making use of this idea, Baker and Matthews propose a sufficient condition for how a thing that exists only in thought could have something be greater than it:

(G)   For anything x that existed only in thought, an otherwise exact same thing that existed both in thought and in reality would be greater (not just greater in thought) than x.

A real boy who has all of the properties that Harry Potter has only in thought would be greater than Harry Potter. So if it is conceivable that a real boy have all of those properties, then it is conceivable that there be someone greater than Harry Potter.

Principle (G) has several attractive features. Perhaps you think that things that do not exist in reality do not have any amount of greatness. Principle (G) provides a way for something to be greater than such a thing without assuming that the thing has any amount of greatness in the first place. Or perhaps you think that some nonexistent things have a fair amount of greatness, even though they do not really exist. If, for example, you think that Harry Potter has a remarkable amount of greatness, then you would not want a principle that implied that any actually existing kid, your bratty little cousin, say, is greater than Harry Potter. Principle (G) doesn't imply this. It says instead that anyone who is just like Harry Potter, except for having his various properties in reality rather than merely in thought, would be greater than Harry Potter.

An Improved Version of the Argument

We saw above that in our initial formulation of Anselm's argument the inference from

(2) For all x, if x does not exist, then it is conceivable that there is something greater than x (premiss)

to

(3) If B does not exist, then it is conceivable that there is a being greater than B (by universal instantiation, where "B" is a name whose reference is fixed by the description "the being than which a greater cannot be conceived")

presupposes that B is one of the things that exists, that it is one of the things within the domain of a general claim made about everything. But if we reject this inference, then we are left without support for

(4) It is conceivable that there is something greater than B.

The proposals that Baker and Matthews give offer an alternative route to (4), one that does not require universal instantiation onto an object whose existence is in dispute. As before, we start with an assumption for *reductio ad absurdum*:

(1') B does not exist in reality. (assumption for *reductio ad absurdum*)

Next we add

> (2')   If B does not exist in reality, then if it is possible for something to have in reality all of the properties that B has in thought, then it is conceivable that there is something greater than B (OES) and (G)

and

> (3')   It is possible that something has in reality all of the properties that B has in thought. (premiss)

Now we can legitimately deduce

> (4)   It is conceivable that there is something greater than B (1') (2') (3')

from these new premisses and then continue the argument, as before, with

> (5)   It is not conceivable that there is something greater than B. (premiss)
>
> ∴   (6)   B exists. (1')–(5), *reductio ad absurdum*

A New Problem Rears Its Head

Now that we have found a way to support (4) that depends on (G), the principle that justifies a comparison of greatness with beings that exist in thought only, we should turn our attention to (5). After all, the same principles of referring to objects of thought and the same standard (G) of comparative greatness should apply to it. According to Baker and Matthews, when we use a name or referring expression in a context where there is disagreement about whether the object exists, then the expression refers to an actual object, if there is one, and it refers to a non-actual, mere object of thought, otherwise. So the name "B" in the context of the dispute between Anselm and his atheist opponent, and thus in the argument, refers to God, if God exists, and if God doesn't exist, then "B" refers instead to the mere object of thought that has-in-thought the property of *being such that it is that than which nothing greater can be conceived.*

Whichever object of thought "B" refers to, given that it is referential, (5) must be interpreted *de re*, that is, as

> (5*)   B is such that it is not conceivable that there is something greater than it.

Since the referent of "B" is either something existing in reality or it is an object of thought existing merely in the understanding, which proposition (5*) expresses depends upon whether God exists in reality. If God does exist in reality, then (5*) expresses the proposition that

(5*r)   *God* is such that it is not conceivable that there is something greater than it.

But if God does not exist in reality, then (5*) instead expresses the proposition that

(5*u)   *The mere object of thought that has-in-thought the property of being such that it is that than which nothing greater can be conceived* is such that it is not conceivable that there is something greater than it.

Now (5*r) seems to me to be true. But, as we have just seen in developing the alternative argument for (4), under the assumption that God does not exist, (5*u) is false. Or, more carefully, the theory that Baker and Matthews produce provides a reason for thinking that (5*u) is false, at least if it is possible that something really has the property of being such that it is that than which nothing greater can be conceived.[10] If B exists only in the understanding but it is possible that something has-in-reality the property of being such that it is that than which nothing can be conceived, then, by (OES), it is possible that there be an otherwise exact same thing as B. But if B exists only in thought and it is possible that there be an otherwise exact same thing as it, then, by (G), B is such that it *is* possible that something be greater than it. In this case, then, B is such that it is conceivable that there is something greater than it.

So the premiss (5*) either expresses the true proposition (5*r), or it expresses the false proposition (5*u). Which one that is, the true one or the false one, depends upon whether the being that which it is not conceivable that there be a greater exists in reality. If we do not assume that God exists, or that "B" refers to an object that exists in reality, we cannot say whether (5*) expresses a truth or a falsehood.

Our first formulation of Anselm's argument foundered for the reason that a crucial inference in the argument presupposed that God exists. We found a way around that problem by appealing to Baker and Matthew's theory of "objects of thought," according to which Anselm and his atheist opponent can both refer, neutrally, without taking a stand on whether or not that object of thought exists. But this strategy leaves it open as to whether a crucial premiss of the argument is true. Thus, the argument is not successful under this interpretation, either.

Notes

1   This exceptionally brief history ignores many philosophers between Kant and the late 20th century who wrote about the ontological argument, and, in particular, it ignores the work of Charles Hartshorne, who anticipated the application of modal logic to interpreting the argument. See, for example, his *Anselm's Discovery* (Hartshorne, 1967).

2   In the 5th century, Augustine had all of the ingredients for thinking of God as the greatest possible being, but his attempt to argue for the existence of such a being is singularly unpersuasive, primarily, I think, because he didn't avail himself of the *reductio ad absurdum* form of argument. See Wierenga (2011).

3   Some philosophers, including Norman Malcolm, think that there is a better argument in the following chapter of the *Proslogion*.

4   Anselm writes "*aliquid quo nihil maius cogitari possit.*" The text quoted above translates this phrase as "something than which nothing greater can be thought," which is a rendering many recent translations adopt. But much of the secondary literature and some other translations use the formulation, "something a greater than which cannot be *conceived*" (cf. Malcolm, 1960, p. 41). I'll follow the latter usage only because it often reads more smoothly and not to mark any distinction.

5   Anselm had quoted the Psalms (13:1, 52:1) "The fool has said in his heart, 'There is no God'" to have an example of someone for whom God exists in the understanding but who denies that God exists in reality. Unfortunately, the derogatory label for Anselm's atheistic opponent stuck; hence its use in Gaunilo's defense.

6   This is how Anselm takes the objection. He says, "[you claim], moreover that what I say *does not follow*, namely, that 'that-than-which-a greater-cannot-be-thought' exists in reality from the fact that it exists in the mind, any more than that the Lost island most certainly exists from the fact that, when it is described in words, he who hears it described has no doubt that it exists in his mind" ("Reply to Gaunilo," in *The Major Works*, chapter 1, emphasis added, Anselm of Canterbury, 1998).

7   Recall that "B" is a name whose reference is fixed by the description "the being than which a greater cannot be conceived."

8   The revised version of Gaunilo's objection is an improvement over the first version not only in proposing an argument of *the same form* as Anselm's. It might be that the conclusion of the original argument, that the greatest island exists, isn't *false*; if one of our actual islands is greater than all the others, the greatest island does exist.

9   This view has some parallels with the account of reference to fictional objects presented by Saul Kripke in his *Reference and Existence* (Kripke, 2013).

10   If it is *not* possible that anything have this property, then premiss (3') of the argument is false.

Suggested Reading

Lynne R. Baker and Gareth B. Matthews, "Anselm's Argument Reconsidered," *The Review of Metaphysics* 64.1 (2010): 31–54.

Peter Millican, "The One Fatal Flaw in Anselm's Argument," *Mind* 113.451 (2004): 437–476.

Graham Oppy, "Ontological Arguments," *The Stanford Encyclopedia of Philosophy* (Spring 2015 Edition), Edward N. Zalta (ed.), http://plato.stanford.edu/archives/spr2015/entries/ontological-arguments.

Alvin Plantinga, *God, Freedom, and Evil* (New York: Harper and Row, 1974; reprinted Grand Rapids, MI: Wm. B. Eerdmans, 1977), pp. 85–112.

4

The Argument from Design

Watches and Watchmakers

In 1802 William Paley (1743–1805), the Archdeacon of Carlisle Cathedral in the north of England, presented what turned out to be an enormously influential example. He wrote:

> In crossing a heath, suppose I pitched my foot against a *stone*, and were asked how the stone came to be there; I might possibly answer, that, for any thing I knew to the contrary, it had lain there forever: nor would it perhaps be very easy to show the absurdity of this answer. But suppose I had found a *watch* upon the ground, and it should be inquired how the watch happened to be in that place; I should hardly think of the answer which I had before given, that, for any thing I knew, the watch might have always been there. Yet why should not this answer serve for the watch as well as for the stone? Why is it not as admissible in the second case, as in the first? For this reason, and for no other, viz. that, when we come to inspect the watch, we perceive (what we could not discover in the stone) that its several parts are framed and put together for a purpose, *e.g.* that they are so formed and adjusted as to produce motion, and that motion so regulated as to point out the hour of the day; that, if the different parts had been differently shaped from what they are, of a different size from what they are, or placed after any other manner, or in any other order, than that in which they are placed, either no motion at all would have been carried on in the machine, or none which would have answered the use that is now served by it. (Paley, 1802, chapter 1)

According to Paley, if you find a watch and notice that its parts fit together and are arranged so precisely as to serve the aim of telling the time, the

The Philosophy of Religion, First Edition. Edward R. Wierenga.

reasonable thing to conclude is that the watch had a designer; the design present in the watch is evidence of a watchmaker. Paley goes on to list some factors that wouldn't weaken this inference even if they were true: you don't know how watches are made and have never seen one made; the watch sometimes goes wrong or is never precisely accurate; there are parts of the watch that don't seem to be required; or someone tells you that the matter in the location where you found the watch had to be arranged in some way or other, and in a watch-like fashion is simply one of many possible ways it could be arranged. Whether any of these conditions hold (and Paley lists a few more), it is, nevertheless, reasonable to conclude that the watch was designed.

Paley then claims that the same kind of inference is available regarding the universe, or at least many parts of it. He writes:

> Every indication of contrivance, every manifestation of design, which existed in the watch, exists in the works of nature; with the difference, on the side of nature, of being greater and more, and that in a degree which exceeds all computation. I mean that the contrivances of nature surpass the contrivances of art, in the complexity, subtlety, and curiosity of the mechanism; and still more, if possible, do they go beyond them in number and variety; yet, in a multitude of cases, are not less evidently mechanical, not less evidently contrivances, not less evidently accommodated to their end, or suited to their office, than are the most perfect productions of human ingenuity. (Paley, 1802, chapter 3)

The conclusion we are supposed to draw is that, just as the design exhibited by a watch justifies us in believing the watch to have had a designer, so the design exhibited by things in the natural order justifies us in believing that nature had a designer, as well.[1] But is there an argument here, and, if so, how exactly is it supposed to proceed? Perhaps we can summarize Paley's detection of design throughout nature as the claim that

    (1) The universe exhibits design.

Maybe we should add

    (2) Everything that exhibits design was designed.

and then deduce

  ∴ (3) The universe was designed. (1) (2)

Paley doesn't actually assert (2), however, and in any event, we shouldn't expect (2) to be widely accepted. But exactly how is (1) supposed to justify (3)?

An Argument from Design

A suggestion can be found in another statement of the argument, given several decades earlier by one of the characters in David Hume's (1711–1776) *Dialogues Concerning Natural Religion* (1779). There Cleanthes says to his companions Philo and Demea,

> Look round the world: contemplate the whole and every part of it: You will find it to be nothing but one great machine, subdivided into an infinite number of lesser machines, which again admit of subdivisions to a degree beyond what human senses and faculties can trace and explain. All these various machines, and even their most minute parts, are adjusted to each other with an accuracy which ravishes into admiration all men who have ever contemplated them. The curious adapting of means to ends, throughout all nature, resembles exactly, though it much exceeds, the productions of human contrivance; of human designs, thought, wisdom, and intelligence. Since, therefore, the effects resemble each other, we are led to infer, by all the rules of analogy, that the causes also resemble; and that the Author of Nature is somewhat similar to the mind of man, though possessed of much larger faculties, proportioned to the grandeur of the work which he has executed. By this argument *a posteriori*, and by this argument alone, do we prove at once the existence of a Deity, and his similarity to human mind and intelligence. (Hume, 1947, part 2)[2]

Cleanthes here claims to *prove* the existence of a Deity; that is, God. But his remark about the "rules of analogy" suggests that we should not think of the argument in question as a *deductive* argument. Rather, the argument from design is best construed as an *inductive* argument. In a valid deductive argument the truth of the premises guarantees the truth of the conclusion; by definition, if an argument is valid, it's not possible for its premises to be true and conclusion false. The argument we were tempted to attribute to Paley is a valid argument:

(1)   The universe exhibits design.
(2)   Everything that exhibits design was designed.
∴ (3)   The universe was designed. (1) (2)

But, as we noted, it would be difficult to secure widespread assent to (2). In contrast, in a good inductive argument, the truth of the premises doesn't guarantee the truth of the conclusion; rather, they *confirm* or *support* or *give a good reason* for the conclusion. For example, the argument

(4) Every emerald we have examined has been green.

Probably,

(5) The next emerald we will examine will be green.

seems like a good inductive argument. Our direct evidence about the green color of emeralds we have examined is also evidence in favor of the proposition that the next emerald we find will also be green. In any event, we should not object to the argument from design simply on the grounds that it is inductive, for the fact is that we (implicitly) rely on inductive arguments in much of our daily lives, for example, in thinking that flipping the switch will turn on the lights, that the food your favorite restaurant serves you is safe to eat, or that the floor will support your weight.

Perhaps, then, the way to turn Paley's claims about the watch and Cleanthes' appeal to the productions of human contrivance into an inductive argument is as follows:

(6) The universe exhibits design that is analogous to the design exhibited by productions of human contrivance.

(7) The design exhibited by the productions of human contrivance is a result of their having been designed.

Probably,

(3) The universe was designed. (1) (2)

Some Initial Objections to the Argument

Hume has his other characters propose objections to the argument defended by Cleanthes. These objections may be divided into two kinds: the first attempt to show that the argument does not succeed in justifying its conclusion; the second, which we will take up in the next section, claim that even if the argument does establish its conclusion, that conclusion is far weaker than the proponent of the argument intends.

No arguments from a part to the whole

Philo asks, "Can a conclusion, with any propriety, be transferred from parts to the whole?" He then adds, "A very small part of this great system, during a very short time, is very imperfectly discovered to us; and do we thence pronounce decisively concerning the origin of the whole?" The suggestion, I think, is that we have only observed a small part of the universe – far smaller in Hume's day than our own, but still relatively small – and even that for only a small fraction of the time the universe has existed. So the part of the universe that we observe exhibits design, but how does that justify us in thinking that the whole universe exhibits design? So understood, this is an objection to the first premiss of the argument, (6). Philo thinks that we do not have enough evidence to support it.

One thing to note is that Philo is certainly correct that one cannot always reason correctly from traits of a part of a thing to a trait of the whole thing. Any part of my car weighs less than 500 pounds, but of course it doesn't follow that my whole car weighs less than 500 pounds. On the other hand, it sometimes is reasonable to argue from a part to the whole. The criminal defendant would not persuade the jury by saying, "I concede that the sample of my blood matches the blood at the scene of the crime; but how do you know that the rest of my blood is like that? You can't argue from a part to the whole." So sometimes a part is representative of the whole, or, as in the example of the blood, the part is a good sample. Is the part of the universe human beings have observed representative of the whole universe? Our actual practice is to think of it that way: we assume, for example, that the speed of light is a constant throughout the universe and not merely in our vicinity. Thus, this first objection is not decisive.

It is worth noting that, even if the objection were convincing, the defender of the argument has a fallback position. The argument could be revised to conclude, not that the whole universe was designed, but that a significant part of it was. It might still be impressive to learn, for example, that our solar system and the Milky Way and other nearby galaxies were designed.

No analogical arguments about unique objects

Philo also claims that analogical reasoning does not hold in the case of unique objects. He says,

> When two species of objects have always been observed to be conjoined together, I can infer, by custom the existence of one whenever I see the existence of the other; and this I call an argument from experience. But how this argument can have place where the objects, as in the present case are single, individual, without parallel or specific resemblance, may be difficult to explain.[3]

Philo adds, "to conclude that an orderly universe must arise from some thought and art like the human ... it were requisite that we had experience of the origin of worlds; and it is not sufficient, surely, that we have seen ships and cities arise from human art and contrivance." Philo admits that some analogical arguments of this style can reasonably support a conclusion, but he claims that such arguments are unsuccessful in a "subject so sublime and so remote for the sphere of our observation," in particular, when the subject is as unique as the universe. What shall we say about this objection? On the one hand, every object is unique or individual in some sense, for example, the next emerald I discover (supposing I discover just one), or the heaviest rock in the field, but we should be able to construct respectable analogical arguments about such objects. Perhaps this is just a superficial kind of uniqueness. Suppose instead that we found a sphere of a completely unknown substance. We would nevertheless be justified in reasoning about it by analogy with similar sized or shaped objects. We could, for example, reasonably assume that the law of universal gravitational attraction applied to it and thus calculate its rate of acceleration if dropped. Finally, we might note that cosmologists who attempt to study the origin of the universe or the nature of the big bang seem to appeal to analogical reasoning to what we may concede are unique objects or events in the sense Philo intends. Of course this isn't a refutation of Philo's claim – perhaps the cosmologists are in trouble, too, or perhaps their arguments are different in some significant way. Still, it is tempting to think that Philo's second objection is no more compelling than his first.

The analogy is too weak

Philo also objects that the analogy between the universe and the human artifacts exhibiting design is too weak to support the conclusion of the argument. He says,

> What I chiefly scruple in the subject ... is not so much that all religious arguments are by Cleanthes reduced to experience, as that they appear not to be even the most certain and irrefragable of that inferior kind. That a stone will fall, that fire will burn, that the earth has solidity, we have observed a thousand and a thousand times; and when any new instance of this nature is presented, we draw without hesitation the accustomed inference, The exact similarity of the cases gives us a perfect assurance of a similar event, and a strong evidence is neither desired nor sought after. But whenever you depart, in the least, from the similarity of the cases, you diminish proportionately the evidence; and may at last bring it to a very weak *analogy*, which is confessedly liable to error and uncertainty.

Philo adds

> If we see a house, Cleanthes, we conclude with the greatest certainty that it had an architect or builder because this is precisely that species of effect which we have experienced to proceed from that species of cause. But surely you will not affirm that the universe bears such a resemblance to a house that we can with the same certainty infer a similar cause, or that the analogy is here entire and perfect. The dissimilitude is so striking that the utmost you can here pretend to is a guess, a conjecture....

And he complains about the "wide step" taken in comparing the universe to "houses, ships, furniture, machines; and from their similarity in some circumstances, [inferring] a similarity in their causes." In other words, Philo is willing to concede:

(6)   The universe exhibits design that is analogous to the design exhibited by productions of human contrivance, and

(7)   The design exhibited by the productions of human contrivance is a result of their having been designed.

But he denies that the analogy between the universe and the productions of human contrivance is close enough or strong enough to support

(3)   The universe was designed.

What should we say about this objection? I think we have to concede that the analogy between the universe and a house is not nearly as close as that between, say, a new house and other houses we have seen. If we find a new house on a lot that was previously vacant and notice that the house exhibits design, we are certainly justified, on the basis of the similarity to other houses, in thinking that the new house had a designer, just like the other houses with which we are familiar. And if we compare the design of the universe to the design of houses, ships, cities, or machines, etc., we certainly do not have the same level of support for the conclusion that the universe was designed.

In fact, we might have no support at all, especially in view of what seems to be an attractive alternative explanation of the design found in nature. For example, although Paley (see note 1) and other 18th-century natural theologians were much impressed by the design exhibited by the human eye, Darwinian evolution proposes that the structures of the mammalian eye developed through the mechanisms of natural selection over the course of millions of years. Hume has an example that can be adapted to make a similar point. He imagines an elegant ship, a "complicated, useful, and beautiful machine," and then argues that we need not attribute ingenuity to the carpenter because he might merely have been "a stupid mechanic who imitated others, and copied an art which, through a long succession of ages, after multiplied trials, mistakes, corrections, deliberations, and controversies, had been gradually improving." (Hume actually uses this example for a point about inferring the nature of the designer, which we'll discuss in the next section.) The impressive beauty of the ship might not be the result of any especially intelligent designer; rather, a long evolutionary process, of trial and error, resulted in the vessel of today. Ships don't reproduce, but the ones that sink don't get replicated.

Perhaps the argument can be improved by appealing to a distinction introduced by Richard Swinburne. He contrasts "regularities of co-presence" with "regularities of succession" (Swinburne, 2004, p. 153). The former are things arranged in a spatial pattern that exhibits design. Paley's watch, Cleanthes's natural machine, subdivided into lesser machines, and the human eye all exhibit regularities of co-presence. Processes that occur over time in a systematic fashion exhibit regularities of succession. The force of the appeal to Darwinian evolution is that it suggests that there can be regularities of co-presence without an actual designer. An example might help. My backyard used to have Chinese elms laid out in a sort of checkerboard pattern. The way the trees lined up exhibited a regularity of co-presence. But no one planted the trees that way. There was no intention on anyone's part to arrange those trees. Rather, the land used to be an orchard. The fruit farmer regularly mowed a crisscross pattern between the peach trees. Wherever a peach tree died, a Chinese elm sprang up. An elm that started to grow anywhere else was cut down by the mowing. But the ones that sprouted in the unmowed squares grew to maturity. There is a further moral to this example, however: although the distribution of the trees was not due to plan or design, the regular mowing – a regularity of succession – not only exhibited design but was itself a designed activity. Similarly, even if the structure of the human eye is due to the processes of natural selection, those very processes exhibit a regularity of succession. Similarly, impressive features of the earth's landscape are the result of regular geological processes, and crystalline structures are the result of systematic chemical processes.

Perhaps, then, the defender of the argument from design can say, first, that the relevant design exhibited by the universe is the regular operation of causal or natural laws or, to use Swinburne's term, its *orderliness*. On this suggestion, to revert to Paley's example, it is not so much that the parts of the watch are put together in a certain order as it is that the arrangement of the watch's parts determines that they *move* in an orderly way. Second, the human planning and construction of the watch proceeds in a way that reflects the patterns of thought that go into that planning and building. More generally, this sort of design is analogous to the regularities of succession involved in intentional human action and temporally ordered human activities, ranging from writing computer programs to performing the ordered notes in a musical composition or improvisation. If we interpret the argument in this way, do the premises provide better support for the conclusion? Do they at least make the conclusion more likely to be true than not? I am not sure what to say. Maybe the premises provide more support for the conclusion than we would have on no evidence at all, but they might not make the conclusion more likely than not. In the next section we can be more definitive.

A Compelling Objection

Hume has his characters present a second line of attack against the argument. According to this objection, even if we concede that the premises of the argument provide (some) support for

(3)   The universe was designed.

they don't provide any support for

(8)   The universe was designed by God.

or

(9)   God exists.

One prong of the attack is to claim, as Philo does, that on the basis of this argument we "have no reason … for ascribing perfection to the Deity." Some things in the universe don't seem to work right, and, in any event, "it is impossible for us to tell, from our limited views, whether this system contains any great faults or deserves any considerable praise." Moreover, even if we could tell that the world is perfect, we might not be justified in attributing this perfection to the designer. The example of the ship made by a "stupid mechanic who imitated others" is supposed to illustrate this point. As Philo puts it, "Many worlds might have been botched and bungled, throughout an eternity, ere this system was struck out; much labor lost; many fruitless trials made; and a slow but continued improvement carried on during infinite ages in the art of world-making." We might not be tempted by the thought that the universe is merely the latest in a long series of attempts to make a good universe. But the question of whether our world, with its suffering, injustices, and natural disasters, was made by an omnipotent, omniscient, and morally perfect God is a serious one, which we will take up in the next chapter. In any event, it does seem that the design actually exhibited by the universe does not justify attributing perfection to whoever designed it.

The second prong of Hume's attack is to note that if the analogy between the universe and the products of human contrivance is really close enough to justify the application of the principle that like effects have similar causes, then it also licenses the further claim that the source of the universe's design is similar in many more respects to human designers than merely being a designer. Philo again:

> And what shadow of an argument … can you produce to prove the unity of the Deity? A great number of men join in building a house or ship, in rearing a city, in framing a commonwealth; why may not several deities combine in contriving and framing a world: This is only so much greater similarity to human affairs. By sharing the work among several, we may so much further limit the attributes of each and get rid of that extensive power and knowledge which must be supposed in one deity.…

In general, the more complicated a product of human contrivance is – Philo mentions houses, ships, and cities; we may add skyscrapers, airplanes, and computers – the more likely it is that it was designed by many people, each working on a part of the project. None of the designers of these things needs to have the really impressive attributes it would take to be able to complete the project single-handedly. Although Philo doesn't mention it, it's also true that the more complicated something is, the more likely it is that it was built by a different group of people from those who designed it. So the premises of the argument also fail to give us a reason to think that there was a single creator of the universe.

Philo continues

> And why not become a perfect anthropomorphite? Why not assert the deity or deities to be corporeal, and to have eyes, a nose, mouth, ears, etc.? Epicurus maintained that no man had ever seen reason but in a human figure; therefore, the gods must have a human figure. And this argument, which is deservedly so much ridiculed by Cicero, becomes, according to you, solid and philosophical.

> In a word, Cleanthes, a man who follows our hypothesis is able, perhaps, to assert or conjecture that the universe arose from something like design: But beyond that position he cannot ascertain one single circumstance, and is left afterwards to fix every point of his theology by the utmost license of fancy and hypothesis.

Philo's claim, then, is that if all we have to go on are the premises of this argument, the analogy of the design of the universe to the design of human productions, we may have some reason to think that the universe was designed, but we can make at best a fanciful conjecture as to who is responsible for that design. Given this analogy, it is at least as likely that the universe had multiple designers and multiple builders, many of whom are no longer alive, who were limited in their knowledge and their skills, and who were embodied, than it is that there is a single designer who is "without a body (i.e. a spirit) who is eternal, free, able to do anything, knows everything, is perfectly good, is the proper object of human worship and obedience, the creator and sustainer of the universe."[4] In sum, the argument from design seems not to show that it is *God* who was the designer.

A New Design Argument: Fine-Tuning

In recent years many philosophers have been impressed with the discoveries of modern physics that show that many of the most basic forces in nature are such that if they had been ever so slightly different, life would have been impossible. Some of these parameters, as listed by Robin Collins (1999, pp. 47–75), are

a. If the initial explosion of the big bang had differed in strength by as little as one part in 10^{60}, the universe would have collapsed back onto itself or expanded too rapidly for stars to form.
b. If the strong nuclear force had been stronger or weaker by 5%, life would be impossible.
c. If gravity had been stronger or weaker by one part in 10^{40}, then stars would not exist.
d. If the electromagnetic force were slightly stronger or weaker, life would be impossible.[5]

These "fine-tuning" features of the universe have inspired philosophers to appeal to them in constructing a new version of the argument from design.

One way of developing such an argument is to appeal to a principle stated in terms of probability, a principle Elliot Sober calls the "Likelihood Principle" (LP):

(LP)   Observation O supports hypothesis H_1 more than it supports hypothesis H_2 if and only if $\Pr(O \mid H_1) > \Pr(O \mid H_2)$.

"$\Pr(O \mid H_1) > \Pr(O \mid H_2)$" is to be read as stating that the conditional probability of Observation O given hypothesis H_1 exceeds the conditional probability of O given hypothesis H_2. If a given observation is more likely to be made if one hypothesis were true rather than a competing hypothesis, the observation supports the first hypothesis.[6]

Let's summarize the fine-tuning features listed above as ABCD, and let us imagine that those features were "observed." Then our observation sentence in this case is

(O_2)   The universe has fine-tuning features ABCD.

The two competing hypotheses are

(U_1)   The universe was created by an intelligent designer.

and

(U_2)   The universe was produced by a mindless chance process.

The argument now proceeds by noting that it's much more likely that the universe would have the fine-tuning features if it were designed by an intelligent designer than if it were the result of a mindless chance process. In other words,

$\Pr(O_2 \mid U_1) > \Pr(O_2 \mid U_2)$

Therefore, according to (LP), the observation of the fine-tuning features of the universe supports the hypothesis that the universe had an intelligent designer more than it supports the hypothesis that the universe was produced by a mindless chance process.

An interesting literature has developed to discuss this argument, with a number of philosophers, including Robin Collins, endorsing some version of it. Rather than engage that literature, however, I want simply to apply the points we made in our discussion of Cleanthes's version of the argument.

Perhaps it is more likely that there was a designer than that the universe resulted from mere chance. But what does that tell us about the nature of the designer? Does it still exist? Is it a spirit who is all-knowing, all-powerful, perfectly good, and someone to whom we owe worship and obedience? I think the bare assertion that there was a designer does not provide an affirmative answer to these questions. Accordingly, the fine-tuning argument seems no more successful as a proof of God's existence than its predecessor.

Notes

1   In fact, Paley does not make this inference immediately. In the intervening sections of his text he marvels at the human eye and eyes in other animals, and he compares them to the lenses of telescopes, before he concludes that the display of contrivance in nature testifies to the "existence, the agency, the wisdom of the Deity."

2   When Cleanthes describes the argument as *a posteriori* he means that our justification for the premises comes "after" experience or evidence. By claiming that we can prove God's existence "by this argument alone" he means to deny that the ontological argument, which we described in Chapter 3 as *a priori*, succeeds.

3   The mention of observation of conjoined species (or kinds) of objects alludes to Hume's account of causation, according to which when we think that one thing causes another, for example, that the fire causes the heat, all we really observe is a constant conjunction between fire and heat and an inclination on our part to expect heat when we observe fire. See Hume (1975), 5.1. Philo's objection could perhaps be put more forcefully if we could assume Hume's theory of causation.

4   This is the passage from Richard Swinburne's *The Coherence of Theism*, rev. ed. (1993), p. 1, we cited in the first chapter to specify what we understood God to be.

5   Collins (1999, pp. 47–75). Collins illustrates the accuracy of one part in 10^{60} by comparing it to "firing a bullet at a one-inch target on the other side of the observable universe, twenty billion light years away, and hitting the target." Collins cites Jefferson Davis (1987), p. 140, as the source of this example.

6   We could have represented Paley's reasoning about the watch in a similar way. Let the observation of the watch be

(O1)   The watch has features XYZ … (parts that fit together, move in a certain way, are capable of keeping time, etc.)

and the competing hypotheses be

(W_1)   The watch was created by an intelligent designer.
(W_2)   The watch was produced by a mindless chance process.

If the watch was produced by a mindless chance process, it would be surprising that it has features XYZ; but if it was produced by an intelligent designer, it would not be surprising that it has features XYZ. If we represent *being surprising* as low conditional probability, we can say that the probability that the watch has features XYZ given that it was produced by a mindless chance process $[\Pr(O_1 \mid W_2)]$ is low. But the probability that the watch has features XYZ given that it was designed by an intelligent designer $[\Pr(O_1 \mid W_1)]$ is not so low. Applying (LP) to the case of the watch, we can conclude that the observation that the watch has features XYZ supports the hypothesis that it had a designer more than it supports the hypothesis that it was produced by a mindless chance process, because $\Pr(O_1 \mid W_1) > \Pr(O_1 \mid W_2)$.

Suggested Reading

Robin Collins, "A Scientific Argument for the Existence of God," in Michael Murray, ed., *Reason for the Hope Within* (Grand Rapids, MI: Wm. B. Eerdmans, 1999), pp. 47–75.

Laura L. Garcia, "Teleological and Design Arguments," in Charles Taliaferro, Paul Draper, and Philip L. Quinn, eds, *A Companion to the Philosophy of Religion*, 2nd edn (Chichester: Wiley-Blackwell, 2010), pp. 375–384.

Elliot Sober, "The Design Argument," in W. E. Mann, ed., *Blackwell Guide to the Philosophy of Religion* (Oxford: Blackwell Publishing, 2004), pp. 117–147.

Richard Swinburne, *The Existence of God*, rev. edn, chapter 8, "Teleological Arguments," (Oxford: Oxford University Press, 2004).

5

The Problem of Evil

Atheistic Arguments

We have seen that the standard arguments for God's existence do not succeed. Is it possible, instead, to prove that God does not exist? There are various ways of trying to argue that God doesn't exist, but many of them are at best superficially promising. Some people seem to think that if you can't prove that God exists then he doesn't exist, or at least one should then think that God doesn't exist. But, in general, from the mere fact that you can't prove something to be true, it doesn't follow that it is reasonable to think that it is false. Here is a familiar example to make this point: Goldbach's Conjecture is the thesis that *every even number greater than two is the sum of two primes.* No mathematician has so far been able to prove it. But it doesn't follow that it is false or that we should think it is false.[1]

Another common way of objecting to theistic belief is to claim that the believer only has the belief that God exists because he or she was born into a particular culture where belief in God was widespread, or because he or she had parents who held that God exists, or because he or she came under the influence of a religious leader.[2] But we are rational in holding very many beliefs that we wouldn't have had if we had been born at different times or in different cultures, for example, that the earth revolves around the sun. So the mere fact that we would have had different beliefs had we been in different circumstances doesn't by itself discredit the beliefs we have. Moreover, this line of reasoning does not really yield an argument that God does not exist. If you tried to formulate this objection as an argument, the conclusion would not be the

The Philosophy of Religion, First Edition. Edward R. Wierenga.
© 2016 Edward R. Wierenga. Published 2016 by John Wiley & Sons, Ltd.

proposition that *God does not exist.* Rather, it would be some claim about the propriety of believing that proposition.[3]

More sophisticated versions of this sort of objection that criticize the source or utility of theistic beliefs include explanations from speculative psychology, sociology, and the cognitive science of religion. For example, Sigmund Freud claimed that religious belief alleviates psychological trauma; Karl Marx thought that religious belief served the aims of the ruling class and was "the sigh of an oppressed people"; Émile Durkheim claimed that religion promoted a "collective consciousness" that had the effect of unifying a society.[4] Pointing out that having religious beliefs has some desirable or undesirable consequences, however, has no bearing on the question of the truth of those beliefs. You could derive real comfort, in perfectly ordinary circumstances, from believing that the floor will support your weight, but that doesn't discredit the belief in the least.

More recently, researchers in the emerging specialty of the cognitive science of religion have attributed religious belief to a hyperactive agency detector in our remote ancestors. On this theory, early humans stood a better chance of surviving in an environment full of predators if they were overly quick to attribute agency behind a rustle in the grass (possibly a venomous snake) or a depression in the sand (possibly the paw print of a nearby and hungry lion). We descendants of those early humans still have an inclination to attribute agency, including supernatural agency, behind events in the natural world.[5] But these more sophisticated theories of the origins or effects of theistic belief do not provide an argument *against* God's existence. For that we will have to look elsewhere.

The Problem of Evil

By far the most serious challenge to belief in God derives from the vast amount of evil the world contains. Even most theists find it troubling that a world created by God would contain pervasive evils. One form this concern can take is to challenge or question God. The figure of Job, in the book of that name in the Hebrew Bible, is someone who asks how God can allow the just to suffer.[6] Concern about evil has thus been part of western theism from nearly the beginning. It is one thing, however, to question God about the presence of evil or to abandon trust in him because of it; it is something else altogether to appeal to the presence of evil to argue against God's existence. But this is precisely what a long philosophical tradition has done.

First, however, a word about terminology: some dictionaries give as synonyms for "evil" such theologically loaded terms as "wickedness" or "sinfulness." If to be wicked or to be sinful requires rebelling against God, then there couldn't be any evil unless God existed. But this is not how the philosophical tradition has used "evil" in this discussion. Rather, in this discussion, evil is whatever is intrinsically bad, bad in itself, or worth avoiding just for its own sake. The contrast is with intrinsic goodness, or whatever is valuable in itself. We can make these ideas a little clearer if we return to the work we were considering in the previous chapter, Hume's *Dialogues Concerning Natural Religion* (Hume, 1947).

When Hume's characters debate a version of the problem of evil, they begin by listing various things that are evil. Demea claims that "the whole earth ... is cursed and polluted. A perpetual war is kindled amongst all living creatures. Necessity, hunger, want stimulate the strong and courageous; fear, anxiety, terror agitate the weak and infirm" (Part X). Philo adds that "Man is the greatest enemy of man. Oppression, injustice, contempt, contumely, violence, sedition, war, calumny, treachery, fraud – by these they mutually torment each other." Then Demea jumps back in with "the disorders of the mind ... remorse, shame, anguish, rage, disappointment, anxiety, fear, dejection, [and] despair...." In a neat science-fiction example, Demea sums up his account: "Were a stranger to drop on a sudden into this world, I would show him, as a specimen of its ills, an hospital full of diseases, a prison crowded with malefactors and debtors, a field of battle strewed with carcasses, a fleet foundering in the ocean, a nation languishing under tyranny, famine or pestilence." These bad things are all examples of what is meant by evil.[7]

After this litany of bad things, Philo returns to what he had earlier described as Cleanthes's anthropomorphism in his argument from design, with the challenge:

> And is it possible, Cleanthes, ... that after all these reflections, and infinitely more which might be suggested, you can still persevere in your anthropomorphism, and assert the moral attributes of the Deity, his justice, benevolence, mercy, and rectitude, to be of the same nature with these virtues in human creatures? His power, we allow is infinite; whatever he wills is executed; but neither man nor any other animal is happy; therefore, he does not will their happiness, His wisdom is infinite; he is never mistaken in choosing the means to any end; but the course of nature tends not to human or animal felicity; therefore, it not established for that purpose. ...
>
> Epicurus's old questions are yet unanswered.
>
> Is he [God] willing to prevent evil but not able? then is he impotent. Is he able, but not willing? then is he malevolent. Is he both willing and evil? whence then is evil?

In the final paragraph of this speech, Philo comes very close to saying that the existence of evil is logically incompatible with the existence of an omnipotent benevolent God.

The Logical Problem of Evil

In a provocative and influential paper published in 1955, the Australian-British philosopher, J. L. Mackie made explicit the objection contained in Philo's concluding paragraph (Mackie, 1955, pp. 200–212). Mackie began by noting that although "the traditional arguments for the existence of God have been fairly thoroughly criticized by philosophers ... the theologian [theist?] can accept this criticism. He can admit that no rational proof of God's existence is possible" (Mackie, 1955, p. 200). Mackie goes on to launch his objection:

> I think, however, that a more telling criticism can be made by way of the traditional problem of evil. Here it can be shown, not that religious beliefs lack rational support, but that they are positively irrational, that the several parts of the essential theological doctrine are inconsistent with one another, so that the theologian can maintain his position as a whole only by a much more extreme rejection of reason than in the former case. He must now be prepared to believe, not merely what cannot be proved, but what can be *disproved* from other beliefs that he also holds. (Mackie, 1955, p. 200)

Mackie summarizes the problem as follows:

> In its simplest form, the problem is this: God is omnipotent; God is wholly good; and yet evil exists. There seems to be some contradiction between these three propositions so that if any two of them were true the third would be false. But at the same time all three are essential parts of most theological positions: the theologian, it seems, at once *must* adhere and *cannot consistently* adhere to all three. (Mackie, 1955, p. 200)

According to Mackie, then, the propositions

(1) God is omnipotent
(2) God is wholly good
(3) There is evil

are contradictory but essential to theism. Let's examine the latter claim first. We have been understanding theism as Richard Swinburne described it, namely, as the claim that that there is a God who is all-powerful, all-knowing, perfectly good, and who is the creator and sustainer of the universe. If to be all-powerful is simply to be omnipotent and to be perfectly good is the same as being wholly good, then it looks as though Mackie is right about (1) and (2) being essential to theism – they're included in what is meant by theism. On the other hand, (3) doesn't seem to be part of the definition of theism, and it also doesn't seem to be essential to God that there be evil – that is, God could exist without there being any evil. Nevertheless, that there is evil is central to the beliefs of the major western theistic religions, Judaism, Christianity, and Islam. These religions agree that the world isn't the way it is supposed to be, that there are wrongs that need righting, that there is suffering, that alms should be given to help others who are in need, or that people stand in need of atonement, for example. In addition, God calls for repentance from sin, which wouldn't make much sense if there weren't any sin, and God offers salvation from sin. So (3) is at least a central tenet of the western religions.

It would be possible to avoid Mackie's objection by giving up (1) or (2), and some believers have done that, sometimes in response to horrific evils they have experienced or are aware of. But this would be to abandon theism.[8] It would be harder to reject (3), if only because (3) is, regrettably, so obviously true. Some people might try to deny (3) by claiming that evil isn't real – there is just *merely apparent* evil. But it would be evil if most of us were deluded about whether there really was evil (even if this didn't rank up there with the world's really great evils); so the view that evil isn't real leads to the conclusion that there really is evil. In any event, our project is to investigate whether Mackie has a good objection to theism, and he seems correct in holding that theists are committed to (1)–(3).

Let's turn, then, to Mackie's claim that (1)–(3) are contradictory. In a straightforward sense a contradiction is the conjunction of a proposition with its denial, for example, any proposition of the form p & not-p. Mackie clearly doesn't mean to claim that any of (1)–(3) are contradictory in this way, nor that that their conjunction is, since none them is the denial of the others. Instead, he intends something a little more intricate. He writes:

> the contradiction does not arise immediately: to show it we need some additional premisses, or perhaps some quasi-logical rules connecting the terms "good", "evil", and "omnipotent". These additional principles are that good is opposed to evil in such a way that a good thing always eliminates evil as far as it can, and that there are no limits to what an omnipotent thing can do. From these it follows that a good omnipotent being eliminates evil completely, and then the propositions that a good omnipotent thing exists and that evil exists, are incompatible. (Mackie, 1955, pp. 200–201)

Before we try to state this, we can reach a better grasp of Mackie's claim if we look at a different example. Consider,

(4)   Mark is a bachelor.
(5)   Mark is married.

There's a sense in which these two propositions are contradictory, even though neither is the denial of the other; they *cannot* both be true. A way of showing this is to note that there is a relevant necessary truth connecting the concepts of being a bachelor and being married, namely,

(6)   Necessarily, anyone who is a bachelor is not married.

With the help of (6), we can deduce a contradiction from (4) and (5). Let's do so.

      (4)   Mark is a bachelor.
      (5)   Mark is married.
      (6)   Necessarily, anyone who is a bachelor is not married.
∴   (7)   If Mark is a bachelor, then Mark is not married. (6) *universal instantiation*
∴   (8)   Mark is not married. (4) (7) *modus ponens*
∴   (9)   Mark is married and Mark is not married. (5) (8) *conjunction*

Now (9) is an explicit contradiction, and we can tell just by looking at it that it can't possibly be true. But if (9) follows validly from (4), (5), and (6), and (6) is a necessary truth (so it can't possibly be false), then it follows that at least one of (4) and (5) is false. They can't both be true.

We can put Mackie's claim in a parallel way: Start with

(1)   God is omnipotent.
(2)   God is wholly good.
(3)   There is evil.

Then add the propositions he calls "quasi-logical rules":

(10)   A good thing always eliminates evil as far as it can.
(11)   There are no limits to what an omnipotent thing can do.

We may concede that it follows from (1)–(3) and (10) and (11) that

(12)   There is no evil,

and thus from (3) and (12) that

(13)   There is evil and there is no evil.

Since (13) is an explicit contradiction and it follows validly[9] from the theistic propositions (1), (2), and (3), supplemented by (10) and (11), it follows that if (10) and (11) are indeed necessary truths, then (1), (2), and (3) can't all be true. So if Mackie's additional principles really are necessary truths, he is right that the three propositions theists believe can't all be true.[10]

Examining Mackie's Charge

Are (10) and (11) necessary truths? Is there no way things could go according to which they are false? It's easy to see that (11) needs revision; there's not much to recommend it as a necessary truth. As we will see in the next chapter, theists typically recognize all sorts of limitations on ability that are nevertheless compatible with being omnipotent. For now it will be sufficient merely to note one such restriction: omnipotence does not extend to what is logically or metaphysically impossible.[11] So let's replace (11) with

(11')   There are no limits, apart from metaphysical impossibility, to what an omnipotent thing can do.

And let's agree, subject to further refinement in the next chapter, that it is a necessary truth. This change actually strengthens Mackie's objection. For if God is omnipotent and can do what is impossible, perhaps he makes contradictions (like (13)) true even though they can't be, and perhaps he has made it the case that the theist's beliefs (1), (2), and (3) are all true even though Mackie has proven that they are not. So adopting (11') as a friendly amendment closes a loophole that could otherwise threaten Mackie's project.

Thinking about (10) is a little more complicated. First, a simple matter: "eliminate" means to get rid of. Strictly, then, a good thing can eliminate evils only if they already exist. But I'm sure that Mackie's idea is that really good things don't let evils on the scene in the first place. Moreover, (10) doesn't specify *when* good things eliminate evil. Maybe they always do, but not immediately. (Compare Augustine's famous prayer, "Make me chaste, Lord, but not yet.") If it is true that God eliminates all evil but hasn't gotten around to it yet, then Mackie won't be able to deduce

(12)   There is no evil.

The most he could derive is that

(12*)   At some time there will be no evil,

which is consistent with the existence of evil now. Perhaps we can avoid both of these problems by recasting (10) as

(10')   A good thing always *prevents* evil as far as it can.

If God prevents an evil, it doesn't have a chance to exist in the first place, and there's no question as to when he does so – it would have to be ahead of time.

These were easy problems to fix, but we still need to determine whether (10') is a necessary truth. I will argue that it is not. People can be good if they fail to prevent an evil through non-culpable ignorance. Sometimes good things fail to prevent evils that they didn't foresee. A fine, upstanding parent, who vigilantly tries to do what is right, doesn't cease to be a good parent if her teenaged son gets into an accident, even though she could have prevented the resulting evil by not letting the son borrow her car. And sometimes a good thing foresees an evil but doesn't know that he or she has the power to prevent it. ("I didn't realize that pressing *that* button would stop the train before it hurtled off the bridge.")

Another problem is that sometimes evils are *justified*, in which case it can be bad to prevent them. We noted above that evils are *intrinsically bad* things, worth avoiding for their own sake. But sometimes evils can be *instrumentally good*, even though they are intrinsically bad; that is, some evils can be required for obtaining or producing certain goods. For example, a parent might let his toddler topple over a few times – with attendant minor pain and anxiety – in order for the toddler to learn to walk. You might think it worth subjecting yourself to the painful care of a dentist in order to keep a happy smile and the ability to masticate. In cases like these, we don't think that someone isn't good for failing to prevent these evils. Of course, the compensating good has to be good enough to justify allowing the evil (or the even worse thing to be avoided has to be sufficiently worse), and there should be no better way of achieving the same good (or avoiding the worse evil).

We can respond to the first of these issues – the fact of limited knowledge – by adding to the list of propositions to which the theist is committed

(14)   God is omniscient.

An omniscient being won't be unaware of potential evils or of how to prevent them. Moreover, it won't make Mackie's objection any less devastating if it turns out that there are four, rather than merely three, things central to theism that can't all be true. The theist is, after all, committed to (14), and we might as well make use of it in trying to develop Mackie's contention.[12]

Let us try to accommodate the second issue, that sometimes evils are justified, by modifying a concept introduced by Alvin Plantinga. Let's say that

> A person S *properly prevents* an evil $E =_{df}$ S prevents E without bringing about a greater evil and without preventing a good state of affairs that outweighs E.

And let us restrict the attempt to formulate a principle connecting goodness and preventing evil to omnipotent and omniscient beings, taking advantage of the fact that such a being won't have serious gaps in ability or knowledge. Accordingly, we can replace Mackie's (10) with

> (10")   An omniscient and omnipotent good thing prevents every evil it can properly prevent.

Now (10") is plausibly thought to be a necessary truth.

Let's review where we are. The theist believes

> (1)   God is omnipotent.
> (2)   God is wholly good.
> (3)   There is evil.
> (14)   God is omniscient.

To these propositions we add the following principles

> (10")   An omniscient and omnipotent good thing prevents every evil it can properly prevent.
> (11')   There are no limits, apart from metaphysical impossibility, to what an omnipotent thing can do.

Can we now deduce a contradiction from these four theistic beliefs and the two additional (necessarily true) principles? It is clear that we cannot. With Mackie's original principles we could deduce

> (12)   There is no evil,

which contradicts (3), the claim that there is evil. But now, with the revised principles, the most that we are entitled to conclude is

(15)   There is no evil that God can properly prevent.

But that is perfectly compatible with there being evil. If this isn't obvious, perhaps an example will help. I once dropped a jar of spaghetti sauce on the kitchen counter. Thanks to Newton's Third Law,[13] sauce flew up to the ceiling, and some of it stayed there. I scrubbed the ceiling as aggressively as I could. At the end, these were both true:

(16)   There is sauce on the ceiling.
(17)   There is no sauce on the ceiling I can remove by scrubbing.

Similarly, (3) and (15) can both be true – there might still be evil even if there is no evil of the kind that God can properly prevent. The conclusion to draw is that we have not been able to substantiate Mackie's claim. We have not been able to use his method to show that the theist holds contradictory beliefs. The project involved trying to find some propositions about goodness and preventing evil that met two requirements: (i) they were necessarily true, and (ii) when added to the propositions the theist believes a contradiction is deducible. The propositions Mackie proposed, (10) and (11), satisfied the second requirement, but they did not satisfy the first. The propositions we came up with, (10") and (11'), seem to satisfy the first requirement, but they do not satisfy the second. It thus turns out to be an immensely difficult task to show that theism is contradictory. In the next section we will consider the project of showing that theism is not contradictory.

The Free Will Defense

We were unable to substantiate Mackie's charge, but that leaves it open, nevertheless, that the existence of evil is inconsistent with theism. Let us simplify Mackie's objection as the claim that

(18)   God is omnipotent, omniscient, and perfectly good

is inconsistent with

(3)   There is evil.

Alvin Plantinga introduced the distinction between a *defense* against the problem of evil and a *theodicy* (Plantinga, 1974, pp. 27–29). A theodicy is the attempt to say what the real reason for evil is. This would obviously require an exceptional amount of insight. A defense, on the other hand, is the attempt to show the logical consistency or the joint possibility of (18) and (3).[14]

A strategy for showing that a pair of propositions is consistent is the following:

> To show that p and q are consistent, find a proposition r such that it's clear that (i) it is possible that p and r are both true, and (ii) the conjunction of (p and r) entails q.

(One proposition *entails* another proposition just in case it is not possible that the first is true and the second is false.) To see how this strategy is supposed to work, consider

> p = There was a hunting party which contained two fathers and two sons, and each hunter shot exactly one unique bird (no two hunters shot the same bird).
> q = The total number of birds shot by members of the hunting party was three.

These two propositions sound inconsistent. (If they don't seem inconsistent to you, please just play along.) You might think that if there were two fathers and two sons in the hunting party then there were at least four members of the party and so at least four birds shot. But now consider

> r = The hunting party consisted of a man, his father, and his son.

The conjunction of p and r is possible: there would be two fathers and two sons in the hunting party if it was as r described it. The conjunction of p and r, however, entails q; if p and r are both true, then the total number of birds shot by the hunting party is three. So p and q are consistent, after all. For this strategy to succeed, r needn't be true or even remotely plausible. All that's required is that it is consistent with p and together with p entails q.

The task of the Free Will Defense is to apply this strategy in the case in which p and q are

> p = God is omnipotent, omniscient, and perfectly good.
> q = There is evil.

Since the rest of our discussion of this topic will appeal to ideas about possibility and necessity, we will take a brief excursus to develop some of those ideas.

A Modal Interlude: Possible Worlds

In Chapter 2 we stated several principles about the modal concepts of necessity and possibility:

(c)   It is possible that a proposition *p* is true (or *p* is possibly true) just in case there is a way things could go according to which, if they went that way, *p* would be true.

(d)   It is possible that a proposition *p* is false (or *p* is possibly false) just in case there is a way things could go according to which, if they went that way, *p* would be false.

(e)   It is necessary that a proposition *p* is true (or *p* is necessarily true) just in case every way things could go is a way according to which *p* would be true.

(f)   It is impossible that a proposition *p* is true (or *p* is impossible) just in case there is no way things could go according to which, if they went that way, *p* would be true.

Sometimes it's easier to think about modal matters if we think of them by reference to *possible worlds*. Possible worlds were discovered by the great German philosopher, Gottfried Wilhelm Leibniz (1646–1716) (Leibniz, 1985). We can think of them as *complete ways things could go*.[15] We have already been thinking of necessity and possibility in terms of ways things could go. Now we add the further idea of a way that is so complete that adding any additional features to it is no longer a way things could go. Here's another way of thinking of it: Begin by considering all of the propositions that are in fact true. These include propositions about what happened in the past, what is going on now, what will happen in the future, and which things exist and what they're like. These propositions describe one way things could be, namely, the way they really are. And these propositions are complete in this sense: adding any proposition not already included results in a collection of propositions that couldn't all be true and so they wouldn't describe a way things could be. All the true propositions thus determine a possible world, *the actual world*. For other ways things could be, think of some ways things could have been different. Someone else could have won the last US presidential election. If that had happened, other things would have been different, too, for example, what the President's last name is and who is sleeping in the White House bedroom. Any such complete way things could go is another possible world. Some ways things could go are radically different: it might have been that there are no people, for example. And some things could not have been different. Every way things could go is a way according to which all triangles have three sides, no bachelor is married, and if p is true and q is true then the conjunction of p & q is true.

Exploiting these ideas, we can recast our principles above in terms of possible worlds:

(c')   A proposition p is possibly true just in case there is a possible world in which p is true.

(d')   A proposition p is possibly false just in case there is a possible world in which p is false.

(e')   A proposition p is necessarily true just in case p is true in every possible world.

(f')   A proposition p is impossible just in case there is no possible world in which p is true.

It is now easy to see why the strategy we stated above,

> To show that p and q are consistent, find a proposition r such that it's clear that (i) it is possible that p and r are both true, and (ii) the conjunction of (p and r) entails q,

works. Mackie's objection isn't that God's existence is impossible. Rather he allows that God exists in some possible worlds and that evil exists in other possible worlds, but he holds that there is no world where both God and evil exist. If we can find a proposition r satisfying the first condition of the strategy, r will be such that it is possible that *God exists* and r is true. That means that there is some possible world in which God exists and in which r is true. Now if the conjunction of *God exists* & r entails there is evil, that means that every world in which *God exists* & r is true is a world in which *There is evil* is true, as well. So if there is a possible world where God exists and r is true, there is a possible world in which God exists and there is evil. Finding a proposition r, then, that satisfies the two conditions shows that there is a world in which both God exists and evil exists. But in that case God's existence is not logically or metaphysically incompatible with the existence of evil.

Back to the Free Will Defense

The leading idea of the free will defense is that the existence of free creatures making morally right choices in situations where it matters is intrinsically good or valuable.[16] One of the things that contributes to the overall value of a possible world is that it has free creatures in it who perform morally right actions. Having people who, for example, help each other, care for others, promote the good, or choose to align themselves with God, contributes to the overall value of a world. Indeed, having such free creatures is a great enough good that it is worth having, even if those free creatures sometimes go wrong or sometimes make bad choices. Sometimes this is put by saying that it is better to have free creatures who sometimes go wrong than it would be to have mere automata that have somehow been programed or determined only to make right choices. According to this account, then, evil in the world is *justified* evil, because it results from the overriding good of having free creatures, a good that couldn't have been obtained without such creatures. As stated, this story seems more like a theodicy; it appears to identify what the real reason for evil is. The free will defense, which only attempts to show the logical compatibility of God and evil, extracts ideas from this story in order to construct a defense.

This might seem to be an unpromising project, however, because the objector can be expected to claim that even if freedom is such a good thing, God could have made free creatures who don't ever do anything wrong. As Mackie puts it,

> if God has made men such that in their free choices they sometimes prefer what is good and sometimes what is evil, why could he not have made men such that they always freely choose the good? If there is no logical impossibility in a man's freely choosing the good on one, or on several, occasions, there cannot be a logical impossibility in his freely choosing the good on every occasion. God was not, then, faced with a choice between making innocent automata and making beings who, in acting freely, would sometimes go wrong: there was open to him the obviously better possibility of making beings who would act freely but always go right. Clearly, his failure to avail himself of this possibility is inconsistent with his being both omnipotent and wholly good. (Mackie, 1955, p. 209)

To answer this question, we should think a little bit about what it would take for God to create someone, leave the person free with respect to a certain action, and have the person make the right choice. Let's consider what would it take for God to be able to make it the case that

(19) Person *S* freely and rightly chooses to do action *A* in circumstances *C*.

For a start, God would have to be able to create *S* with free will and with the ability to perform *A*, and God would have to be able to place *S* in circumstances *C* and have it be the case that in *C* it would be right for *S* to perform *A*. This much seems easy to arrange. But, according to the free will defender, God couldn't do all of that and also *cause S* to do *A*, for, if God caused *S*'s action, *S* wouldn't be free, after all.[17] And thus by causing *S* to do *A*, God wouldn't be arranging for (19) to be true, after all. Whether God can arrange for (19) to be true also depends on *S*, or on what *S* would do in those circumstances. More precisely, it depends on which of these further propositions is true:

> (20)   If God were to create *S* and leave *S* free in circumstances *C* (in which performing *A* is right), *S* would freely perform *A*.
> (21)   If God were to create *S* and leave *S* free in circumstances *C* (in which performing *A* is right), *S* would freely refrain from performing *A*.

If (20) is true, God could easily arrange for *S* to freely choose *A* in *C*; all God would have to do is create *S* with free will, place *S* in *C*, and then stand back and watch *S* perform *A*. But if (21) were true and God created *S* with free will and placed *S* in *C*, *S* would *not* freely do *A*, and so (19) would not be true. Note, furthermore, that (20) and (21) aren't up to God. If God could somehow first make (20) true and then make *S* and put *S* in *C*, *S* wouldn't be free with respect to *A* – what *S* would do would already have been determined by God.

What's true for person *S* and action *A* is true for every possible person and every potential action. Whether God can arrange for someone freely to do a certain thing depends on something outside of his control, namely, which "counterfactuals of freedom," those propositions like (20) and (21) that specify what free agents would do in various circumstances, are true.[18] But what if every person it's possible for God to create is such that if that person were created by God to have free will, he or she will do at least one wrong action? Then God couldn't create a world containing free persons who always freely choose what's right.

To see how this could happen, consider a simplified case. Suppose you're in a book club with ten other members, the members vote on what books to read, and the only way to have a book considered is to propose it to the group. You would like the group to read your favorite novel, *Tess of the d'Urbervilles*. Now consider these propositions:

If you were to propose to read *Tess*, Member$_1$ would freely vote no.
If you were to propose to read *Tess*, Member$_2$ would freely vote no.
If you were to propose to read *Tess*, Member$_3$ would freely vote no.
If you were to propose to read *Tess*, Member$_4$ would freely vote no.
...
If you were to propose to read *Tess*, Member$_{10}$ would freely vote no.

Each of these propositions is *contingent*; that is, it is true in some possible worlds and false in others. Moreover, they are logically independent of each other. If the members of the group are free agents, there is no logical reason why they should always agree with each other. So every possible combination of truth value of these propositions is also possible. That is, any number of them could be true, with the rest false. One possibility, then, is that they are all true. But if they were all true, then you couldn't get any of the members of the group to freely vote to read *Tess*.[19] So it's possible that you are not able to get any of the members to agree to read your favorite book.

Now let's expand the case a bit so that it represents the situation confronting God before he creates anyone. Let's suppose that he is considering what the various possible free persons he could make would do if he were to create them and leave them free. He might face a list of propositions like this:

> If God were to create person$_1$ and leave that person free, that person would perform at least one wrong action.
> If God were to create person$_2$ and leave that person free, that person would perform at least one wrong action.
> If God were to create person$_3$ and leave that person free, that person would perform at least one wrong action.
> If God were to create person$_4$ and leave that person free, that person would perform at least one wrong action.
> ...
> If God were to create person$_\infty$ and leave that person free, that person would perform at least one wrong action.

As in the case of the propositions about the members of your book club, these propositions are all contingent. A person who freely does something wrong in one possible world can be wholly upright and blameless in another possible world. And these propositions are logically independent of each other: that one person will do something wrong doesn't entail that anyone else will. So, again, every possible combination of truth values – truth or falsity – of these propositions is possible. One of the very many ways the truth values of these propositions can line up is that they are all true. That's a possibility. But if that possibility were actual, God would not be able to create any free creatures at all without getting some wrong-doing, and hence, some evil, in the process. So it's possible that God could not create free creatures who never go wrong. If this possibility were actual, that wouldn't count against God's omnipotence, because omnipotence doesn't require him to be able to perform the impossible action of forcing people to freely do what he wants, and it is similarly compatible with his omniscience. Moreover, actually creating some free persons, if this was the situation God found himself in, wouldn't count against his perfect goodness, as long as the resulting evil was justified by a significant amount of good. So the following proposition (inspired by Plantinga's treatment) seems to be possible and also compatible with God's existence:

> $r=$ A world with free persons and a balance of good over evil is better than a world without free persons; and every possible free person would, if created, perform at least one wrong action; and God has created some free persons.

That is, the conjunction of

> $p=$ God is omnipotent, omniscient, and perfectly good

and r is consistent. But that conjunction entails

> $q=$ There is evil.

Proposition r satisfies the strategy the free will defense employs to show a pair of propositions to be consistent. Accordingly, the existence of God *is* consistent with the existence of evil, and Mackie's claim that it is not has been shown to be mistaken.[20]

Some Loose Ends: Earthquakes, Tsunamis, and Animal Suffering

The free will defense explicitly addresses the existence of *moral* evil; that is, evil that results from the free actions of creatures. But Hume's list of evils included famine, pestilence, and other natural scourges. Other Enlightenment philosophers were much impressed by the Lisbon earthquake and subsequent tsunami of 1755, a natural disaster in which tens of thousands of people lost their lives. Voltaire (1694–1778), for example, used the example of the Lisbon earthquake in his *Candide* (1759) to make fun of Leibniz's contention that this is "the best of all possible worlds." We could no doubt add many more recent disasters and plagues to this list. Let's call such evils *natural* evils. Considering such natural evils suggests an obvious objection to the free will defense: although it shows that moral evils are compatible with the existence of God, it doesn't show that natural evils are. Of course, Mackie's original objection was that *no* evil is compatible with God's existence, so if moral evils are compatible with God's existence, then we have a sufficient reply to Mackie. But it would also be important to discover whether the natural evils of earthquakes, floods, tsunamis, plagues, etc., are compatible with the existence of God. It would not be enough to reply to Mackie's specific objection if there were an equally pressing objection waiting in the wings.

Alvin Plantinga's response to this objection is to suggest that, for all we know, natural evils result from the free actions of Satan and his cohorts, doing their best to make the world nasty. On this suggestion, what we take to be natural evils are actually moral evils, because they, too, result from the free actions of (non-human) agents. If it really is possible that non-human creatures are the cause of the world's diseases and disasters, then it is easy enough to revise proposition *r* so as to use the same strategy to show that God's existence is compatible with the existence of natural evils. Define "broadly moral evil" as evil resulting from the free actions of any agent. Then try:

r' = A world with free persons and a balance of good over evil is better than a world without free persons; and every possible free person would, if created, perform at least one wrong action; and God has created some free persons, both human and non-human; and all the evil in the world is broadly moral evil.

If r' really is possible, then it seems to be compatible with God's existence, and it entails that there is evil but that it's all broadly moral evil. So the evils not caused by human beings are also compatible with God's existence.

Many philosophers have found that it strains credulity to think that earthquakes and other natural evils are caused by devils or demons. But the strategy doesn't require the proposition *r* to be credible or plausible. To establish the logical point, it merely needs to be compatible with the proposition that God exists and in conjunction with the latter to entail that there is evil (or that there is both moral and natural evil).

Still, there is some reason to be suspicious about whether r' really is adequate. Although some natural disasters might seem like freak events that could have been caused by an agent, many such events seem to result from natural *processes*, that is, as a result of the regular operation of causal laws. Would the theist really think it possible that all such processes are due to the agency of Satan? A related issue is the evil of animal suffering. Surely the pain that animals experience when they are preyed upon or injured is to be included among the world's evils, and yet it doesn't seem possible that all such suffering is systematically caused by non-human agents.[21]

A different suggestion about natural evils has been made by several philosophers, including Richard Swinburne and Peter van Inwagen (see Swinburne, 1998, chapters 9–10; van Inwagen, 2006). They point out the value of having natural laws, of having the world operate in regular and predictable ways. One benefit of this regularity is that it seems to be required for significant exercise of free will. There are regularities that relate the force of a falling rock with a certain mass and density to the effect of contact with human tissue. We can count on these regularities to provide an incentive to avoid being in the path of falling rocks. But we can also count on them if we wish to do evil and harm someone. If the regularities held only when no one could get hurt, or if God intervened to prevent causal laws from having their usual consequences any time someone intended to harm another, not only would the world be extraordinarily confusing, but we would never notice anything bad resulting from our vilest efforts. According to van Inwagen, it is a good thing that there are various kinds of animals, including higher-order animals with degrees of consciousness. On his view, it would be an inevitable result of the complex natural laws required for this kind of diversity of life that animals suffer. Again, perhaps God could intervene in every case to prevent such suffering, but in that case the laws would be "massively irregular," and having laws like that would be worse than not having animals. These reflections suggest the alternative proposal for r:

> r'' = A world with free persons, diversity of life forms, and a balance of good over evil is better than a world without free persons; every possible free person would, if created, perform at least one wrong action; God has created some free persons; significant freedom and diversity of life forms requires the regular operation of causal laws; and natural evil results from the regular operation of causal laws.

Now r'' seems compatible with God's existence, and in conjunction with the latter it entails that there is both moral and natural evil. So, by appealing to r'' the free will defender can argue that God's existence is compatible with the existence of both moral and natural evil.

The Evidential Problem of Evil and Skeptical Theism

Largely as a result of the work of Plantinga and the other philosophers we have just been discussing, most philosophers have tended to concede that the logical problem of evil is a failure – the free will defense shows that the existence of God and the existence of evil are logically consistent. But this has led to formulations of the argument from evil as an evidential or inductive or probabilistic objection. The core idea here is the claim that although the existence of evil is compatible with God's existence, the presence of evil provides good evidence against God's existence, or the presence of evil shows that God's existence is unlikely. There is a large and growing body of work on this topic, but we will only be able to scratch the surface here.[22]

Many undergraduates first encounter a version of this objection in a well-known paper by William Rowe, frequently anthologized, and sometimes cited, as "The Inductive Problem of Evil" (Rowe, 1979). There Rowe presents the following argument:

(22) There exist instances of intense suffering which an omnipotent, omniscient being could have prevented without thereby losing some greater good or permitting some evil equally bad or worse.

(23) An omniscient, wholly good being would prevent the occurrence of any intense suffering it could, unless it could not do so without thereby losing some greater good or permitting some evil equally bad or worse.

∴ (24) There does not exist an omnipotent, omniscient, wholly good being. (1) (2) (p. 336)

Since Rowe intends this argument to be valid (although without some fine-tuning, it isn't in fact formally valid) and, hence, deductive, the question arises as to where the inductive reasoning comes in. Following our earlier usage, let's call evil that cannot be prevented without thereby losing some greater good or permitting some equally bad or worse evil, "justified" evil. Then Rowe's argument is really another version of the logical problem of evil, with the difference being that that it is *unjustified* (or "pointless") evil that Rowe claims both exists and is incompatible with the existence of God. So, to repeat, where is the inductive reasoning? The answer, I suggest, is that Rowe thinks that we have inductive evidence in support of the first premiss of the argument.

Rowe gives the example of a fawn, trapped in a forest fire and which "lies in terrible agony for several days before death relieves its suffering." (It is crucial to the example that no one be aware of this evil, for otherwise it might be justified by leading to a good change in someone's behavior.) Rowe claims that, "as far as we can see, the fawn's suffering is pointless," and it could easily have been prevented by an omnipotent, omniscient being. So, Rowe claims, it is likely that there is pointless evil that could have been prevented by God, without losing out on a greater good or bringing about a worse evil. Rowe adds that even if there is a justifying reason for the fawn's suffering, "we must then ask whether it is reasonable to believe … [this] of *all* the instances of seemingly pointless human and animal suffering that occur daily in our world." His answer is that it "seems quite unlikely that all the instances of intense suffering occurring daily in our world are intimately related to the occurrence of greater goods or the prevention of evils at least as bad; and even more unlikely should they somehow all be so related, [that] an omnipotent, omniscient being could not have achieved at least some of those goods … without permitting the instances of intense suffering that are supposedly related to them" (Rowe, 1979, pp. 337–338).

In later papers Rowe gives several slightly different formulations of his objection. One version begins with the claim

(P)   No good we know of justifies an omnipotent, omniscient, perfectly good being in permitting [the evil of the fawn's intense suffering],

from which Rowe infers, inductively,

(Q)   No good at all justifies an omnipotent, omniscient, perfectly good being in permitting [the evil of the fawn's intense suffering].

From the latter, Rowe deduces

(not-G)   There is no omnipotent, omniscient, perfectly good being.[23]

The crucial claim for Rowe is the contention that (P) makes (Q) probable.[24]

In recent years a popular reply to this kind of argument has become known as "skeptical theism." This response agrees that, for very many evils, we are not in an epistemic position to discern or to specify the greater goods for which they are required (or for what greater evils they are required to avoid). But it holds that nothing follows about whether these evils are not appropriately related to some greater goods or worse evils. Skeptical theism is thus skeptical about our ability to identify God's reasons for allowing particular evils, or about what possible goods they are related to that would justify them. Given our epistemic limitations, our failure to discern a good linked in the right way to these evils makes it no more likely that there is none than that there is.

In response to the first version of Rowe's objection, the skeptical theist will simply claim that our inability to say for what good the fawn's suffering was required does not support the claim that there is none.

Accordingly, the skeptical theist will not be persuaded by Rowe's first premiss, (22), the claim that there are unjustified evils.

In response to the second version of Rowe's objection, the skeptical theist might want to quibble about

(P)   No good we know of justifies an omnipotent, omniscient, perfectly good being in permitting [the evil of the fawn's intense suffering].

Maybe there is a good that we are aware of but what we don't know is that it is related in the right way to justify God's permitting the suffering. In that case, the theist might be willing instead to accept

(P')   No good we know of is such that we know that it justifies an omnipotent, omniscient, perfectly good being in permitting [the evil of the fawn's intense suffering].

In any case, the skeptical theist will deny that (P) or (P') provides any support for

(Q)   No good at all justifies an omnipotent, omniscient, perfectly good being in permitting [the evil of the fawn's intense suffering].

Again, just because we don't see the justification doesn't give us a reason to think that there isn't any. As Plantinga has said, "Why suppose that if God does have a good reason for permitting evil, the theist would be the first to know? Perhaps God has a good reason, but that reason is too complicated for us to understand. Or perhaps he has not revealed it for some other reason" (Plantinga, 1974, p. 10).

An Objection and a Reply to Skeptical Theism

There is a large and growing body of literature on the topic of skeptical theism, but we don't have space to consider very much of it.[25] One of the most challenging objections to skeptical theism, I think, is the charge that it leads to skepticism about matters of morality more generally. If we have no idea whether there is some good that God is aware of and that justifies him in permitting a certain instance of suffering, then we would be rash indeed if we attempted to prevent that suffering. If the instance of suffering serves God's purposes, we should, for that reason, allow it to occur. If, as skeptical theism alleges, we have no idea whether a given instance of suffering is needed for a good that God sees and intends, then we should also have no idea whether we should act to prevent that instance. Bruce Russell puts this objection forcefully in the following passage involving an onlooker to an evil:

> ...let us suppose ... that even after failing to find sufficiently weighty moral reasons to justify God's allowing, say, the brutal rape, beating, and murder of a little girl, we are not justified in believing that there are none. It will follow that we are also not justified in believing that some human being who could easily have stopped the heinous crime did something wrong in failing to intervene, After all, the same reason that justifies God in not intervening, if God exists, may be the reason why the human onlooker should not have intervened. (Russell, 1996, pp. 193–205)

And William Hasker makes a similar point with respect to our own moral choices:

> Our judgments about such things [to recognize instances of good and evil and to discern the logical and causal connections between events] ... play a crucially important role in our everyday existence. For us to seriously adopt a skeptical or agnostic attitude about such matters would have serious consequences for our moral lives. (Hasker, 2004, p. 51)

Hasker concludes that skeptical theism leads to "a radical skepticism which would have very serious consequences for our moral reasoning in general."

I think it is possible, contrary to what Hasker claims, to be skeptical about whether there are any instances of intense suffering that God could have prevented without losing a greater good (or permitting an equally bad or worse evil) without having to be skeptical about all moral reasoning.

We should admit at the outset that for many of our moral choices a certain humility is appropriate, independent of considerations of skeptical theism. This is because part of what is involved in making a moral choice is choosing from among the alternative actions open to us; typically that will require recognizing what those alternatives are and at least some consideration of what would happen on each alternative and how good or bad that would be.[26] We make our judgments about the likely outcomes of our actions and the likely value of those outcomes with less than full knowledge, but we nevertheless assume that we arrive at a reasonable belief sufficient to justify our acting.

When we make moral choices, we must do so within the context of what we are able to predict about the outcome of our actions. If it seems to me that my action will prevent an instance of intense suffering without eliminating a greater good or bringing about an equal or worse evil (and I have no alternative action with even better consequences) then I am typically justified in thinking that it is right for me to prevent that suffering. But since I realize that my predictions about the future and my grasp of what goods there are and how they are related to my actions are restricted by my cognitive limitations, I am in no position at all to judge what someone else, not so limited, would be justified in doing. In particular, if I believe that God can see (infinitely) far into the future, that he has a perfect grasp of what goods there are, and that he has a perfect knowledge of the relevant connections between them, I should conclude that I have no idea what will seem best to God. For all I can tell, by looking further into the future and by having a vastly better understanding of good and evil, God does discern a great good that requires an instance of suffering and which justifies him in not preventing that suffering.

A second difference between our situation and God's is more striking. As we have seen, a moral agent chooses, at a time, from a set of alternative actions open to the agent at that time. Naturally enough, different agents, even at the same time, have different sets of alternatives, depending upon differences in their abilities, their knowledge, their strength, their locations, and, more generally, in the circumstances in which they find themselves. If one of my alternatives is better than anything else I can do, it might not even be one of your alternatives. In that case, perhaps I ought to do it, but you need not (because you cannot). And even if it is one of your alternatives, you might have an even better action open to you that is not open to me. In that case, it would be better for you to do something else, even if it would not be better for me to do something else. It is obvious that the alternative actions open to God are vastly different from the alternatives open to us. We cannot even begin to imagine most of the actions available to God. Given this, the skeptical theist's claim that we do not know what God ought to do seems fairly plausible; since our knowledge of what he is able to do is so limited, we are not in a position to judge what he ought to do. But skepticism about what is the best among God's options should not lead to skepticism about our own; our own alternatives are typically familiar, the kinds of things we and other people are used to thinking about. So, I can hold reasonable beliefs about what I should do, even though I am ignorant of what God should do.

In the passage quoted above, Russell seems to assume that if preventing an instance of intense suffering is something I can do, then it is surely something that God can do. But if he is not preventing the suffering, then it must be something that he wants, and so I should not prevent it, either. Perhaps *preventing the suffering* is indeed one of God's alternatives but *allowing the suffering so that I can prevent it* is another of God's alternatives and is in fact a better alternative, for whatever reason, to his preventing the suffering himself. Of course, allowing the suffering so that I can prevent it is not one of my alternatives. So it could turn out that preventing the suffering is the best alternative open to me, but that there is a better one open to God. I should not use the fact that he seems not to be preventing the suffering as a reason not to do so myself. So being skeptical about God's reasons for allowing evil need not lead to skepticism about our own moral choices.

Notes

1   A harder question is whether it is okay to believe Goldbach's Conjecture. We'll consider whether it's rational to believe a proposition that you can't prove to be true in Chapter 11.

2   For an interesting discussion of the relevance of "epistemic luck," for example, the circumstances into which one is born, to the rationality of belief see Baker-Hytch (2014).

3   Alvin Plantinga in *Warranted Christian Belief* (Plantinga, 2000) distinguishes between *de jure* and *de facto* objections to theistic belief. *De jure* objections allege that belief in God is unjustified or irrational or otherwise suspect. The objection that the believer only believes because his or her parents did is, according this terminology, *de jure*. An argument for the conclusion that God does not exist would be a *de facto* objection – it would be an argument against the *fact* that God exists. According to Plantinga's own theory, if God exists, then the typical believer is *warranted* in believing that he does. *De jure* objections allege that the typical believer is not warranted. It follows, then, that any successful *de jure* objection is automatically a *de facto* objection. This claim depends upon Plantinga's unique theory of warrant – that which is required for true belief to count as knowledge – which he defines in terms of the proper functioning of our epistemic faculties. I'll consider Plantinga's theory in Chapter 11. I am leaving it open, however, that a *de jure* objection could fail to be a *de facto* objection.

4   See, for example, Sigmund Freud, *The Future of an Illusion* (1964 [1927]) and Émile Durkheim, *The Elementary Forms of the Religious Life* (1976 [1912]). Marx's most famous remarks on religion were contained in the Introduction (1843) to his projected but never completed *Contribution to the Critique of Hegel's Philosophy of Right*. That Introduction was published the following year in the sole issue of a journal Marx co-edited.

5   For a much richer example of the cognitive science of religion, see Pascal Boyer, *Religion Explained: The Evolutionary Foundations of Religious Belief* (Boyer, 2001).

6   The text dates perhaps to the 6th century BCE. Both Jews and Christians accept it as part of the Bible. In addition, the Qur'an lists Job as among the prophets. Thus, all three western monotheisms evince an early concern with the place of evil in a world made by God.

7   A hedonist about value who holds that only suffering, pain, or unhappiness is intrinsically evil will want to be more precise here. On that view, many of the items on Hume's list are only bad because of the pain and suffering to which they typically lead – disease and the other things are *instrumentally* bad but not intrinsically bad. I won't be concerned with these details except to note that when we come to the free will defense I will assume that *people freely making morally good choices* is an intrinsic good – so I will assume, against hedonism, that there are more things that are intrinsically good than happiness or pleasure.

8   Compare Richard Rubenstein in *After Auschwitz: Radical Theology and Contemporary Judaism* (Rubenstein, 1966), who argues that, in the wake of the Holocaust, Jews could no longer believe in an omnipotent God who acts in history. My remark that to give up (1) or (2) is to abandon theism is not intended as criticism of the position but as description. Our question in this chapter is whether there is a good objection to theism; we won't be able to answer this question by either endorsing or rejecting theism.

9   At any rate, let us stipulate that this inference is valid. (10) and (11) need a little polishing to make the inference *formally* valid.

10 At this point it should become apparent, if it wasn't already, to readers familiar with Plantinga's *God, Freedom, and Evil* just how indebted I am to that work. In fact that book influences much of the present volume but perhaps nowhere more so than on the topic of evil.

11 For an example of a major figure who held that omnipotence does not require the ability to do the impossible, consider this remark of Aquinas, "If, however, we consider the matter aright, since power is said in reference to possible things, this phrase, *God can do all things*, is rightly understood to mean that God can do all things that are possible; and for this reason He is said to be omnipotent" (Aquinas, 1948 [1485], *Summa Theologiae* Ia, 25, 3).

12 Recall that in Philo's presentation of the objection quoted above he includes the claim that God's "wisdom is infinite; he is never mistaken in choosing the means to any end," which is an appeal to divine omniscience.

13 For every action, there is an equal and opposite reaction.

14 In *The Problem of Evil* (van Inwagen, 2006), Peter van Inwagen introduces a slightly different concept of defense, namely a story that might, for all we know, be true and according to which both God and evil exist. For van Inwagen, then, a defense offers not merely a metaphysical possibility but an *epistemic* possibility.

15 For an influential work that takes possible worlds to be complete ways things could be (i.e. as maximally consistent states of affairs), see Alvin Plantinga, *The Nature of Necessity* (Plantinga, 1974). For a radically different but also influential conception of worlds, see David Lewis, *On the Plurality of Worlds* (Lewis, 1986).

16   One source of this idea is St. Augustine (354–430 CE). See his *On Free Choice of the Will* (Augustine, 1993). In this work Augustine was interested in a slightly different question, not whether the existence of God and evil were compatible, but how it could happen that a world that was created by a wholly good God could end up containing evil or how evil could somehow proceed from God. His answer was that it was good for God to make creatures with free will, even if they sinned against him.

17   The free will defense as usually developed presupposes *incompatibilism*; that is, the thesis that free action is incompatible with there being antecedent causally sufficient conditions for the action's being performed. I think that incompatibilism is true. But a majority of contemporary philosophers accept *compatibilism*, according to which an action can be free, even if it is caused, as long as those causes are of the right kind. Typically compatibilists agree that being caused to perform an action by a nefarious neurosurgeon manipulating you through electrodes implanted in your brain, or less dramatically, by the grip of an addiction, is the wrong kind of cause for you to be free with respect to that action. But the usual causes of our actions, our beliefs and desires, for example, are the kinds of causes that leave actions free.

Is the free will defense available to a compatibilism? In my "Review of James Tomberlin and Peter van Inwagen (eds.), Alvin Plantinga," (Wierenga, 1988), I claimed that being caused by God to perform an action is one of the wrong kinds of cause and thus not compatible with acting freely. So even if some antecedent causes are compatible with free action, God can't make creatures freely perform the actions he wants. Recently Jason Turner (2013) has given a detailed development of this idea. Turner argues that God's creating a world in which causal determinism is true would not allow him to get creatures who freely did what he wanted – if God took into account what the initial conditions and causal laws he established would determine, the creatures would not be free; and if he didn't know what the conditions and laws would determine, he couldn't be sure of getting a world he wanted. If this is right, the compatibilist can agree with the structure of the free will defense as presented in the text, demurring only at some of the details.

18   The free will defense thus appeals to Molinism, a theory developed by Luis de Molina (1535–1600). Molina held that God has knowledge of these counterfactuals of freedom and that they are independent of his will. He called this knowledge "middle knowledge." A good introduction to Molina's thought can be found in *Of Divine Foreknowledge (Part IV of the Concordia)* (Molina, 1988). An excellent recent presentation and defense of Molinism is Thomas Flint's *Divine Providence: The Molinist Account* (Flint, 1998). We will appeal to some Molinist ideas again in Chapter 8, "A Somewhat More Complicated (But Compelling) Objection to the Argument."

19   I made the simplifying assumption above that the only way to get the members of the group to freely choose to read a book was by proposing it. In real life, you could consider offering a bribe or other inducement. Accommodating these additional options would make the example needlessly complicated.

20 Mackie's objection was that the existence of God and the existence of evil are not compatible. It is therefore appropriate to reply to that objection by arguing that the existence of God is compatible with *some* evil. But the objection could have been developed differently. Perhaps you think that God could co-exist with some evil but not with the vast quantity of evil we actually have, or not with certain kinds of especially despicable evil, or not with evil distributed in evidently unjust ways. It is beyond the scope of this book to consider all of these variations on Mackie's objection. Plantinga addresses some of them in *God, Freedom, and Evil*. Here is an exercise left to the reader: formulate alternative versions of the objection and find an appropriate r for each.

21 The pain of domestic animals that are abused by human beings falls under the category of moral evil. I have in mind here, primarily, the suffering of animals in the wild. For two recent discussions of the problem of animal suffering, see Dougherty (2014) and Murray (2008).

22 A good way into the literature is to begin with the essays in Daniel Howard-Snyder, *The Evidential Argument from Evil* (Howard-Snyder, 1998).

23 See, for example, "The Evidential Argument from Evil: A Second Look," in Howard-Snyder (1998), pp. 262–285.

24 I have focused on a couple of versions of Rowe's version of the evidential problem of evil and have not mentioned variations of the objection that are explicitly probabilistic. In "The Evidential Argument from Evil: A Second Look," Rowe himself develops the argument in Bayesian terms. And Paul Draper has argued that the probability that pleasures and pains are distributed in the way they actually are is much higher on the hypothesis that no supernatural being is responsible for the condition of sentient beings than it is on the hypothesis that God exists. Accordingly, the actual distribution of pleasure and pain is better explained by the "hypothesis of indifference" than it is by the existence of God. See his "Pain and Pleasure: An Evidential Problem for Theists" (Draper, 1989, pp. 331–350). Skeptical responses to these versions of the argument will add a skepticism about some of the relevant probabilities. It is beyond the scope of this chapter to discuss these additional issues.

25 See, for example, Dougherty and McBrayer (2014).

26 One need not be a thoroughgoing consequentialist to view moral reasoning in this way; for example, even W. D. Ross in *The Right and the Good* (Ross, 2002 [1930]) recognized the prima facie duties of *beneficence* (promoting the good) and *non-maleficence* (not promoting evil), and the Kantian question of whether one can consistently will a maxim to be a universal law requires considering the effects of everyone acting on that maxim.

Suggested Reading

Marilyn McCord Adams, *Horrendous Evils and the Goodness of God* (Ithaca, NY: Cornell University Press, 1999).

Daniel Howard-Snyder, *The Evidential Argument from Evil* (Bloomington and Indianapolis, IN: Indiana University Press, 1996).

J. L. Mackie, "Evil and Omnipotence," *Mind* 64 (1955): 200–212.

Alvin Plantinga, *God, Freedom, and Evil* (New York: Harper and Row, 1974; reprinted Grand Rapids, MI: Wm. B. Eerdmans, 1977), pp. 7–64.

Eleonore Stump, *Wandering in Darkness: Narrative and the Problem of Suffering* (Oxford: Oxford University Press).

Peter van Inwagen, *The Problem of Evil* (Oxford: Oxford University Press, 2006).

6

Omnipotence

Divine Attributes

We have looked at three major arguments in favor of God's existence, and
we have investigated the most important argument against God's existence.[1]
Now we'll turn to an examination of some of the divine attributes. We have
been guided in our discussion by Richard Swinburne's formula: theism is
the thesis that there is someone "without a body (i.e. a spirit) who is eternal,
free, able to do anything, knows everything, is perfectly good, is the proper
object of human worship and obedience, the creator and sustainer of the
universe." This gives us several attributes to look at. First, we'll attempt to
understand the property of *omnipotence* ("able to do anything"), and we'll
consider an objection that alleges that the very concept is incoherent. Then
we'll look at *omniscience* ("knows everything"), and we'll examine the claim
that divine omniscience is inconsistent with something many of us take to
be true, namely, that we sometimes act with free will. Finally, we'll consider
an objection that two of the divine attributes, *perfect goodness* and *perfect
freedom* are inconsistent with each other. Thus, in addition to trying
to understand these attributes, we'll consider three different kinds of objections that have been raised against them.

Attributing Omnipotence

There is a long philosophical tradition, going back at least to Augustine,
continuing through the major medieval Jewish, Christian, and Muslim
philosophers, and extending up to the present, of attributing omnipotence to

The Philosophy of Religion, First Edition. Edward R. Wierenga.
© 2016 Edward R. Wierenga. Published 2016 by John Wiley & Sons, Ltd.

God. But why is there this consensus that omnipotence is one of the divine attributes? The term "omnipotent," after all, seems to be a philosophical invention. There are, I think, at least three sources for the idea that God is omnipotent. The first is that it is a familiar religious belief, even if it is often expressed in different language. The Bible, for example, does not mention omnipotence, but it does use an apparent synonym, "almighty" (or, rather, Hebrew and Greek words accurately translated as "almighty"). For example, Exodus 6:2–3 reports that "God also spoke to Moses and said to him: I am the LORD. I appeared to Abraham, Isaac, and Jacob as God Almighty, but by my name, 'The LORD' I did not make myself known to them." And a passage in the New Testament book of Revelation (19:6b), "Hallelujah! For the Lord our God the Almighty reigns," is perhaps better known for its adaptation by Handel in *The Messiah*, "For the Lord God Omnipotent reigneth...." This attribution, moreover, is not limited to the Jewish or Christian traditions: one of the 99 names for God in Islam is "*Al-Muqtadir*," The Powerful.

A second source of the idea that God is omnipotent derives from "perfect being theology." Although Anselm's ontological argument, as we saw, does not succeed as a proof, his thought that God is "that-than-which-nothing-greater-can-be-conceived" has had a pervasive influence. Anselm's formula, that God is whatever it is better to be than not, yields the result that having power is a great-making property, one that contributes to the greatness of a being. The greatest possible being will therefore have the greatest amount of power. Finally, reflection on Swinburne's description, "the proper object of human worship" (Swinburne, 1993, p. 1) can lead to the conclusion that a being who deserves to be worshiped should be extraordinary, including having unlimited power.

Defining Omnipotence and an Objection

The etymology of the word "omnipotent," in which the root "*omni*" means *all*, and "potent" comes from "*ponens*," meaning *powerful*, suggests that omnipotence may be understood by quantifying over *all* items of some sort and then attributing power with respect to those things. For example, omnipotence might have to do with all tasks or with all abilities. Or perhaps it could be defined by reference to all actions, as in

(D1)   A being, S, is omnipotent $=_{df} S$ can perform any action A.

To be omnipotent, according to (D1) is to have the ability to do absolutely anything.

If this is right, it is easy to see a strategy for raising an objection to God's being omnipotent, namely, just find something that he can't do. Homer Simpson seems to have had this in mind when he said, "Hey, I got a question for you. 'Could Jesus microwave a burrito so hot that he himself could not eat it?'"[2] The suggestion is that if Jesus could not, there is something he couldn't do, namely, make a burrito that hot; but if he could, there is something else he couldn't do, namely, eat it. In fact, this is a variation on a standard objection to divine omnipotence, the Paradox of the Stone. Since we are discussing *God's* omnipotence (and not Jesus') and since the philosophical literature mentions stones, let's consider a version of that more familiar formulation:

(1) Either God can create a stone which God cannot lift, or God cannot create a stone which God cannot lift.

(2) If God can create a stone which God cannot lift, then he is not omnipotent (since he cannot lift the stone in question).

(3) If God cannot create a stone which God cannot lift, then he is not omnipotent (since he cannot create the stone in question).

∴ (4) Therefore, God is not omnipotent. (1) (2) (3)[3]

The first premiss of this argument is hard to deny. And the second and third premisses seem initially plausible. Accordingly, it looks like we have an argument that shows that God is not omnipotent. And since "God" in the argument could be replaced with any other name, the argument, if successful, could be revised to show that no one else is omnipotent, either.

But this is a little too quick. You will recall that early in the last chapter I noted that many classical theists denied that God could do just anything. Here is how Thomas Aquinas put it:

All confess that God is omnipotent; but it seems difficult to explain in what his omnipotence precisely consists. For there may be a doubt as to the precise meaning of the word "all" when we say that God can do all things. If, however, we consider the matter aright, since power is said in reference to possible things, this phrase, *God can do all things*, is rightly understood to mean that God can do all things that are possible; and for this reason he is said to be omnipotent. (Aquinas, 1948 [1485], *Summa Theologiae* I, 25, a. 3)[4]

Aquinas seems to be suggesting that we adopt a revised definition of omnipotence:

(D2) S is omnipotent $=_{df}$ S can do any action A that is metaphysically possible.

If we accept (D2) instead of (D1) we have a basis to criticize the argument. We can say that the third premiss is false, on the grounds that *creating a stone that God cannot lift* is an impossible action. (Let's assume that a metaphysically possible action is one that it is metaphysically possible that someone do, and an impossible action is one that it's not possible that anyone do.) If *creating a stone that God cannot lift* is an impossible action, then God doesn't, according to (D2), have to be able to do it in order to be omnipotent. Hence, when (3) says that if God can't do it then he is not omnipotent, (3) is mistaken. So the argument, according to this view, is unsound.[5]

If for any possible world God is able to lift any stone there is, there's no possible world containing a stone that God cannot lift. In that case, creating such a stone is an impossible action. Thus far the reply seems promising. The problem is that there are many other actions that *are* possible and which God cannot do. Reformulating the argument by reference to any of them will result in a version of the argument to which the present reply is not available. For example,

> *creating a stone that its maker cannot lift*, and
> *building a house that its builder cannot lift*

are both possible actions. I could build a small doghouse, for example, and it wouldn't take the addition of very many boards and shingles before I would be unable to lift the house. So the second of these two is a possible action. Now if God could lift any possible stone, he could also lift any possible house. But then he couldn't build a house that its builder cannot lift.

Accordingly, we could rewrite the argument using this example. Then the third premiss would be

> (3*)   If God cannot build a house that its builder cannot lift, then he is not omnipotent (since he cannot build the house in question).

In this case, however, we cannot appeal to the impossibility of the action in question to argue for the falsehood of (3*). So we will have to look harder for a resolution of the Stone Paradox. This is not simply a desperate or *ad hoc* maneuver, however, since (D2) is inadequate in any event. Consider the action of *authoring a book whose sole author is Bertrand Russell*. This is a possible action, as we can verify by noting that Russell himself performed it repeatedly. But it can't be done by anyone else, not even God. Yet there is no reason to think, as (D2) requires, that God would have to be able to perform this action in order to be omnipotent.

Doing the Impossible

Before we proceed, we should pause to consider two related issues involving doing the impossible. First, why not simply allow that God *can* do what is impossible? As Harry Frankfurt has pointed out, if it is impossible for God to create a stone he cannot lift but God can do the impossible, then not only can he make such a stone but, having made it, he could proceed to do another impossible action and lift it (Frankfurt, 1964). More generally, if God can do what is impossible, then even if the Stone Paradox argument is sound, he can make it the case that its conclusion is nevertheless false. This strategy gives us a short-cut solution to many of the issues we are discussing. If divine foreknowledge of human actions is incompatible with their being free, then if God can do what's impossible, he can both have foreknowledge and allow people to be free. Or if divine freedom is incompatible with divine perfection, that won't matter, either. If God is not limited to what it is possible, he can have both perfections.[6] I wish that I could refute the view that an omnipotent God can do what is impossible. But the best I can come up with is the claim that if he can, then we could never be certain that the conclusion of a sound argument wasn't false. But this assumes that we don't have any reason to think that God would never exercise that ability, and it ignores the fact that we often can't be certain in any event that an argument we think is sound really is.

Sometimes people claim that God can do what is impossible because they think that it is required for true piety. That seems mistaken, at least if Augustine, Anselm, and Aquinas, or Saadia Gaon and Maimonides, or Avicenna and al-Ghazālī (pick your favorite tradition) were properly pious. But others think that omnipotence requires the ability to do what is impossible because they think that there is a pure or intuitive concept of omnipotence that we can analyze and see that it includes the ability to do what is impossible. Analyzing an intuitive or naïve concept – whether *omnipotence*, *knowledge*, or *free will* – can be an interesting project.[7] But it is not our project. The classical theists admitted so many limitations on ability that they thought were compatible with being omnipotent that they cannot have had an intuitive or naïve concept in mind. Our project, in the first place, is to investigate whether there is a sensible way of understanding the property the classical theists intended when they attributed it to God to characterize his immense power but which also allowed for a range of limitations on ability. In the second place, our project is to consider whether such a conception is subject to philosophical objections, in particular, to the objection posed by the Stone Paradox argument.

Constructing a Definition

Let's begin again in our attempt to construct a definition of omnipotence. If we start with an example of divine power, we might be inclined to frame the definition differently. "*Fiat lux.*" According to Genesis, in the beginning God said, "Let there be light," and there was light. One idea suggested by this example is that what God did was make a certain proposition true, namely, the proposition *There is light.* I said above that defining omnipotence seems to require attributing ability with respect to all of *some* kind of thing. (D1) and (D2) did it by referring to performing *actions*. But let's try *propositions* instead. Then we can think of omnipotence as requiring the ability to make propositions true.

A second idea suggested by this example is that not just any way of making a proposition true is relevant. In the case of making *There is light* true, God did it directly, just by willing that it be true or decreeing that it be true. This second feature is important to emphasize, I think, because someone with a compliant, omnipotent friend could arrange for lots of propositions to be true, just by asking the friend. But this sort of ability should not count as omnipotence. In stories of the genie in the lamp, the person who rubs the lamp gets what he or she wishes (or not, as those stories often go) and thus could be said to make certain propositions true, but it is the genie who has the power, not the person who asks the genie.[8]

So let's try thinking of omnipotence in terms of the ability to directly make a proposition true. Omnipotence, however, should not include the ability to make just any proposition true. For example, the proposition *No one ever directly makes a proposition true* is not one that anyone *could* directly make true; so we shouldn't expect omnipotence to require that ability. Presumably necessarily true propositions also can't be made true. There's nothing anyone has to do in order for *All triangles have three sides* or *7+5=12* to be true. Aquinas' claim that omnipotence extends only to what is *possible* suggests that omnipotence does not include the ability to directly make impossible propositions true, either. So the inability to make *Some triangles have four sides* or *7+5=13* true is no liability. We can summarize these first three exceptions as the claim that

(a)   An omnipotent being need not have the ability to directly make a proposition true if it is not possible that anyone directly make it true.

We have embarked on the task of excluding some categories of propositions from among those that an omnipotent being is able to make true. Let's consider some of the things that various classical theists said in this regard before adding to the list. Augustine claims that God is unable to die or be deceived, and he concludes that God "cannot do some things for the very reason that he is omnipotent" (Augustine, 1950). Anselm adds that God "cannot be corrupted, or tell lies, or make the true into the false (such as to undo what has been done)" (Anselm of Canterbury, 1998, Proslogion, VII). Aquinas gives a lengthy list of things God cannot do, including moving, failing, tiring, making the past not to have been, making himself not to be, and making what he did not foreknow that he would make (Aquinas, 1975, *Summa Contra Gentiles*, I, 2, 25). The 10th-century Jewish philosopher, Saadia Gaon, spoke of "those absurdities that cannot be ascribed to divine omnipotence, such as the bringing back of yesterday and causing the number five to be more than ten" (Saadia, 1948). And in the 12th century, Moses Maimonides wrote,

> That which is impossible has a permanent and constant property, which is not the result of some agent, and cannot in any way change, and consequently we do not ascribe to God the power of doing what is impossible. No thinking man denies the truth of this maxim; none ignore it, but such as have no idea of Logic.... [I]t is impossible that God should produce a being like Himself, or annihilate, corporify, or change himself. The power of God is not assumed to extend to any of these impossibilities.... (Maimonides, 1904, Pt I, chapter 15)

Several of these philosophers mention not being able to do what is impossible. Our condition (a) captures that idea. A second common theme is that, as Augustine puts it, there are some things God cannot do precisely because he is omnipotent. Aquinas' examples of failing or tiring fall under this category. Anselm's example of telling lies falls under this category, too, but the reason needs to be made explicit. His idea, I think, is that God is essentially morally good, and someone like that cannot tell a lie. We can summarize this theme with the condition

(b) An omnipotent being need not have the ability to directly make a proposition true if doing so is incompatible with that being's essential properties.[9]

Other divine attributes may properly limit divine omnipotence. Being morally perfect limits the ability to do some wrong things. And if omniscience (as we will discuss in the next chapter) includes foreknowledge, then it seems clear, as Aquinas says, that God can't make something that he didn't foreknow that he would make. According to (b), he wouldn't have to be able to do that in order to be omnipotent. Earlier we noted that God couldn't author a book whose sole author is Bertrand Russell. Since God has essentially the property of *not being identical to Bertrand Russell*, and having this property is incompatible with authoring a book whose sole author is Bertrand Russell, (b) handles this example, too.

Among the absurdities that Saadia lists is "the bringing back of yesterday," and Anselm and Aquinas concur that God cannot "undo what has been done." This suggests a final condition:

> (c)   An omnipotent being need not have the ability to directly make a proposition true if doing so is incompatible with what has already happened.

Perhaps changing the past is just a special case of doing what is impossible, but stating (c) explicitly allows us to recognize another point: some things are possible to do but it is now too late to do them. For example, it is now too late for God to bring Moses into existence for the first time, even though doing so is possible and compatible with God's essential properties. An adequate account of omnipotence should not require that ability. One way of trying to capture the idea of being compatible with the past is to appeal to the concept of *the history of the world at a time*. It is not easy to make this idea precise, but perhaps we can grasp it anyway.[10] Suppose that you went out to see a movie last night, but you could have stayed home and read. Your going to see the movie and your staying home are each compatible with the history of the world up until last night. In the actual world you went to see a movie, but there is another world, nearly indistinguishable from the actual world up until last night, in which you didn't go to see the movie. The actual world and the other world, we can say, *share a history* up until last evening. They were as alike as could be up until the time you decided to go to the movie. Many of the same propositions are true in both worlds – but not all. In the actual world the proposition that you were going to see a movie last night was true last week, but it wasn't true last week or ever in the second world. In the actual world it was true 80 years ago that God knew that you would see a movie last night, but this wasn't true in the second world, either. In general, two worlds can share a history up until a time without having the same propositions about what happens after that time true in both. Finally, the history of a world up until a certain time is simply what it has in common with other worlds with which it shares a history.[11]

Drawing on the idea of the history of a world and the three conditions, (a), (b), and (c), we can propose the following definition of omnipotence:

> (D3)   *S* is omnipotent in a world *W* at a time $t =_{df}$ *S* is able at *t* in *W* to directly make true any proposition *p* such that *S*'s directly making *p* true at *t* is metaphysically compatible with the history of *W* up until *t*.[12]

If *S's directly making p true at t* is logically compatible with the history of *W* up until *t*, then it is compatible with what has already happened. And if *S's directly making p true at t* is compatible with something, it is possible.[13] Finally, if *S's directly making p true at t* is possible, it also follows that directly making *p* to be true is compatible with *S*'s essential properties and that *p* itself is possible. Thus, the various conditions (a), (b), and (c) are all satisfied.

(D3) incorporates the limitations on ability that classical theists have taken to be compatible with omnipotence. Accordingly, it sets considerably weaker standards for omnipotence than either (D1) or (D2). But does it require enough? Or are the standards it sets too low? One thing to notice is that it isn't easy to be omnipotent according to (D3). You and I don't qualify, for example. An easy way of seeing this is simply by noting that there are all sorts of things compatible with the past that are possible for us to us to do but which we are unable to do. In my own case, such things might include singing *The Star-Spangled Banner* with no false notes, sinking a jump shot from the half court line, or remembering all of the lyrics to *Tangled Up In Blue*.[14]

Back to the Stone

With (D3) in hand, let us see what we can say about the Stone Paradox Argument. That argument, you recall, goes like this:

(1) Either God can create a stone which God cannot lift, or God cannot create a stone which God cannot lift.

(2) If God can create a stone which God cannot lift, then he is not omnipotent (since he cannot lift the stone in question).

(3) If God cannot create a stone which God cannot lift, then he is not omnipotent (since he cannot create the stone in question).

∴ (4) Therefore, God is not omnipotent. (1) (2) (3)

We should recast the premisses in the terms favored by our new definition of omnipotence. So the second and third premisses become

(2') If God can at *t* directly make true the proposition *There is a stone God cannot lift*, then he is not omnipotent.

(3') If God cannot at *t* directly make true the proposition *There is a stone God cannot lift*, then he is not omnipotent.

One unusual thing about (2'), perhaps more apparent now that we've added a temporal index "at *t*," is that it asserts that if at a certain time God is merely *able* to make it true that *There is a stone God cannot lift*, then he is *already* not omnipotent – even if he hasn't in fact made that proposition true or made such a stone. Should we think that is right?

Whether we should or not depends on how we answer a different question. We've used, above, the distinction between *essential* properties and (although I didn't use the term) *accidental* properties. An essential property of a thing, *being identical to Socrates*, or *being self-identical*, is a property the thing cannot exist without having. An accidental property of a thing, *having Plato as a student*, or *being snub-nosed*, is a property a thing could lack. Socrates couldn't have failed to be Socrates, but he could have failed to have had Plato as a student and he could have had a differently shaped nose. There's another, slightly different, distinction that can be made. Some properties are such that if you ever have them, you can't lose them. Other properties are ones you could have for a while and then no longer have. Let's call the former property an "enduring" property.[15] Ernest Hemingway famously said, "If you are lucky enough to have lived in Paris as a young man, then wherever you go for the rest of your life, it stays with you, for Paris is a moveable feast" (Hemingway, 1964). That seems right, for if you ever live in Paris, then *having lived in Paris* is an enduring property for you. But *living in Paris* is not an enduring property for anyone; for anyone who lives in Paris could move away (or be moved).[16]

Now let's ask whether omnipotence is an enduring property for anyone who has it. Suppose it is not. Suppose that God could be omnipotent but then give it up. One way he could give it up would be to make a stone too heavy for him to lift. On this suggestion, he would, while omnipotent, be able to directly make *There is a stone God cannot lift* true; but if he did, he would no longer be omnipotent. As long as he is careful not to do that, however, he would remain omnipotent. On the assumption that omnipotence is not enduring, then, (2') is false. From the assumption that God *can* do something which is such that if he did it he would not be omnipotent, it does not follow that he is *already* not omnipotent.

What if omnipotence is enduring for God? This might strike you as the more plausible position. Garrison Keillor has a short story in which Hera's divorce lawyer confronts Zeus, who asks,

> "What does she want?"
> "She wants what's right. Justice. She wants half your power. No more, no less."
> "Divide power? Impossible. It wouldn't be power if I gave it up." (Keillor, 1995, p. 35)

Perhaps it wouldn't really be omnipotence if it could be given up. Perhaps omnipotence is enduring for anyone who has it. Suppose that's right. According to (D3), (3') is true only if God's directly making true the proposition *There is a stone God cannot lift* at a certain time *t* is compatible with the history of the world up to *t*. But God's directly making that proposition true at *t* is compatible with the history of the world up to *t* only if God is already not omnipotent before *t*. If God is omnipotent before *t*, his being omnipotent is part of the history of the world prior to *t*, and that history is not compatible with God doing something to lose his omnipotence – on the assumption we have made that omnipotence is enduring. So directly making true the proposition *There is a stone God cannot lift* is compatible with the history up to *t* only if God is already not omnipotent prior to *t*. In other words, (3') is true – on the assumption that omnipotence is enduring – only if God is not omnipotent. That is, under this assumption, it follows from (3') by itself, without the assistance of the rest of the argument, that God is not omnipotent. Without some strong reason to accept (3'), it seems inadequate to show that God is not omnipotent.

In sum, if omnipotence is not enduring for God, then (2') is false and the argument is unsound. If omnipotence is enduring for God, then (3') itself presupposes the conclusion of the argument and without a compelling defense is insufficient to establish the conclusion. Either way, the argument fails.[17]

Notes

1   If you think that three arguments in support of God's existence but only one against is unbalanced, the objections to be considered in this and the following two chapters can all be easily turned into arguments against God's existence.
2   Well, maybe he didn't have anything in mind – he is, after all, just a character in a television cartoon, *The Simpsons*. The quotation is from a program that first aired on April 7, 2002.
3   If you are tempted to think that it's simply silly to debate arguments involving burritos or stones, you might prefer J. L. Mackie's version (in "Evil and Omnipotence," 1955) that he calls the "Sovereignty Paradox," which begins by asking whether God can create a creature he cannot control. That seems more serious and also more theologically relevant. But the important evaluative points can be made with any version of the argument, so we will continue with the familiar example of the stone. Notice, also, that there is no actual paradox here. It is just an *argument* against God's being omnipotent.

4   Some other examples (from among Islamic philosophers): Avicenna claims that "one rightly says that power over what is impossible and over what, in itself, does not possibly exist … [is] absurd" (Avicenna, 2009, Book III, chapter 11). And according to al-Ghazālī, "…the absurd is not within God's power. And what is absurd is the simultaneous affirmation and denial of the same thing, or the *affirmation of the specific while denying the more general*, or the affirmation of two things while denying one of them. But what does not reduce to such a case is not an absurdity and therefore is within God's power" (*Tahāfut al Falāsifa*, quoted in Goodman (1992), p. 186).

5   This response to the argument was given by George Mavrodes in "Some Puzzles concerning Omnipotence" (Mavrodes, 1963b).

6   I will argue in the following chapters that these pairs aren't really incompatible. My point here is that if God can do the impossible, we can simply conclude that there is no problem without going to the trouble of working through the details.

7   See, for example, Conee (1991).

8   The example of the genie assumes that the genie acts freely and thus wouldn't have to grant the wish. There is another application of the idea that omnipotence consists in directly making propositions true. We saw (by which I mean, I claimed) in Chapter 5, that God couldn't cause or directly make it true (for a given person, action, and set of circumstances) that

   (i)   *S freely performs A in C.*

It is possible that God could *arrange* for (i) to be true, provided that it was true that

   (ii)   If God were to create S and leave S free in circumstances C, S would freely perform A.

But if it were true instead that

   (iii)   If God were to create S and leave S free in circumstances C, S would freely refrain from performing A

then God could not arrange for (i) to be true, but this would not count against his omnipotence. An implicit assumption in this account is that omnipotence has to do with what a being is able *directly* to make true.

9   A property P is essential to a thing x if and only if it is not possible that x exist but lack P. This condition is equivalent to saying that a thing doesn't have to be able to do what is impossible for *it* to do in order to be omnipotent.

10   I have tried in a couple of places to add some details to the concept of the history of a world by appealing to Plantinga's idea of the *initial segment* of a world at a time. See Wierenga (1989, pp. 18–20; 2011).

11 If this account seems suspiciously circular, perhaps it is. I don't claim to be able precisely to define the concept of the history of a world up until a time, but only to illuminate it. Considering worlds that share a history helps us grasp the concept of a history.

12 (D3) is subject to the objection that the right-hand side of the definition is trivially satisfied by a thing, an inert object, say, that can't possibly directly make any proposition true (since such a thing is able to directly make true *every* proposition such that its directly making that proposition true is compatible with the history of the world *when there are no such propositions*). To avoid this objection we could add a second clause to the definition: "and there is some proposition *p* such that *S*'s directly making *p* true at *t* is logically compatible with the history of *W* up until *t*." Since the objection is technical and the repair easy, I won't bother including the additional clause in the text.

Another potential problem with (D3) is that it refers to abilities at different times. But a traditional view is that God is eternal and outside of time. (For a discussion of this view in the context of divine foreknowledge, see Chapter 7) According to this traditional view, it might not make sense to attribute abilities to God at various times, so it might not be clear that (D3) can apply to God. I think that the best way to respond to this concern is to try to preserve the insights of (D3) but to reformulate it so that it applies to an atemporal being. For one attempt to do this, for a slightly different principle, see Wierenga (1989), pp. 33–35.

13 A state of affairs *S* is compatible with a state of affairs *S'* if and only if it is possible that *S* and *S'* both obtain. If it is possible that *S* and *S'* both obtain, then it is possible that *S* obtains.

14 A more complete defense of this point would give some examples explicitly in terms of directly bringing about the truth of propositions, but that would require that we settle complicated matters in the theory of action. It is plausible to think, however, that whenever we directly cause something to be the case (without doing so by means of causing something else, as when I cause the window to be broken by first causing the ball to move) we directly cause a proposition to be true. To use a philosophical term of art, whenever we perform a "basic action" we directly cause a corresponding proposition to be true. And surely there are examples of this kind that are compatible with the past yet which are such that we are nevertheless unable to make them true – and that's all it takes for us to fail to be omnipotent according to the standard set by (D3).

15 More formally, *P* is an enduring property for $x =_{df}$ (i) it is possible that *x* has *P*, and (ii) necessarily, for every time *t*, if *x* has *P* at *t*, then *x* has *P* at every later time at which *x* exists.

16 Any property that is essential for someone is an enduring property – you can't lose a property you can't exist without having. But not all enduring properties are essential – it's possible that Hemingway never left Oak Park and thus never acquired the property of *having lived in Paris*.

17   It is common in discussions of omnipotence to consider the fictional McEar (or some similarly limited character), who is essentially unable to do anything except scratch his ear. Such inventions are taken to make trouble for proposed definitions like (D3) on the grounds that McEar *is* able to directly make true every proposition that's possible for him to make true (given the history of the world) but he is *not* omnipotent. I myself do not believe that McEar is possible, and I do not think that, in general, a philosophical thesis can be refuted by appeal to an impossibility. I have not had much success in convincing others of this. See, for example, Sobel (2009), pp. 365–366. Others sympathetic to McEar include Wielenberg (2000), and Leftow (2009).

I leave to the reader as exercise the task of figuring out whether appeal to an essentially limited creature who can do everything it is possible for it to do provides a counterexample to (D3) and, if it does, the further task of repairing (D3) to avoid the objection.

Suggested Reading

Brian Leftow, "Omnipotence," in Thomas P. Flint and Michael C. Rea, eds, *The Oxford Handbook of Philosophical Theology* (Oxford: Oxford University Press, 2009), pp. 167–193.

Richard Swinburne, *The Coherence of Theism*, 2nd edn, chapters 9 and 14 (Oxford: Clarendon Press, 1993).

Edward Wierenga, *The Nature of God: An Investigation into Divine Attributes*, chapter 1 (Ithaca, NY: Cornell University Press, 1989).

7

Omniscience, Foreknowledge, and Free Will

Attributing Omniscience

To know everything is to be omniscient. One source of the attribution of omniscience to God derives from the numerous biblical passages that attribute vast knowledge to him. Thomas Aquinas, in his discussion of the knowledge of God (Aquinas, 1948 [1485], *Summa Theologiae*, I, 14) cites such texts as Rom. 11:33 ("O the depths of the riches and wisdom and knowledge of God!"), Job 12:13 ("With God are wisdom and strength; he has counsel and understanding."), and Heb. 4:13 ("And before him no creature is hidden, but all are naked and laid bare to [his] eyes ...").

In addition, as we noted in the last chapter, reflection on what is required to be a perfect being yields the conclusion that such a being possesses all perfections. Presumably this includes not only unlimited power, but also perfect wisdom (as Anselm put it) or unlimited knowledge. Finally, the requirements of certain theological doctrines provide a third source of the idea that God is omniscient. Prominent among these is the doctrine of divine providence, which holds that God has a plan for the world according to which all things are in his care and work out according to his good will. In Thomas Flint's formulation, "to see God as provident is to see him as knowingly and lovingly directing each and every event involving each and every creature toward the ends he has ordained for them" (Flint, 1998, p. 12). It is hard to see how God could order things according to such a detailed plan without having vast, if not unlimited, knowledge.

The Philosophy of Religion, First Edition. Edward R. Wierenga.
© 2016 Edward R. Wierenga. Published 2016 by John Wiley & Sons, Ltd.

Defining Omniscience

We saw in the last chapter that defining omnipotence turns out to be more complicated than one might initially have thought. By contrast, defining omniscience should be much simpler.[1] Knowledge is of propositions, and only truths can be known; so all knowledge is just knowledge of all true propositions. Thus,

(D1) S is omniscient $=_{df}$ for every proposition p, if p is true then S knows p.

We don't have to add anything about *false* propositions, because for every false proposition there is a true one corresponding to it. If q is false, then anyone who knows all truths will know *not-q* or *It's not the case that q*, and this ensures that anyone who knows all truths knows everything.[2]

The true propositions include propositions about the past (*It was a dark and stormy night*), about the present (*Somewhere birds are singing*), and about the future (*You will regret this later*). So a being who is omniscient knows everything about the past, the present, and the future. This last claim is controversial. But it is a consequence of (D1) that if there are truths about the future, an omniscient being has complete *foreknowledge*.

Foreknowledge and Free Will

The reason it is controversial that omniscience includes foreknowledge is that many philosophers have thought that foreknowledge and human free action are incompatible. Boethius (480–524 CE) wrote,

> There seems to be a hopeless conflict between divine foreknowledge of all things and freedom of the human will. For if God sees everything in advance and cannot be deceived in any way, whatever his Providence foresees will happen, must happen. Therefore, if God foreknows eternally not only all the acts of men, but also their plans and wishes, there cannot be freedom of will; for nothing whatever can be done or even desired without its being known beforehand by the infallible Providence of God. If things could somehow be accomplished in some way other than that which God foresaw, his fore-knowledge of the future would no longer be certain. Indeed, it would be merely uncertain opinion, and it would be wrong to think that of God....
>
> Just as when I know that a thing is, that thing must necessarily be; so that when I know that something will happen, it is necessary that it happen. It follows, then, that the outcome of something known in advance must nec-essarily take place. (Boethius, 1962, Book 5, prose 3; cf. Augustine, 1993)

The last sentence suggests the general structure of an argument that Boethius might take to show that divine foreknowledge is incompatible with human free action. Let *S* be any person and *A* any action:

(1) If God foreknows that *S* will do *A*, then *S* must necessarily do *A*.

(2) If *S* must necessarily do *A*, then *S* will not do *A* freely.

∴ (3) If God foreknows that *S* will do *A*, then *S* will not do *A* freely.

Since *S* and *A* can be any person and action, respectively, this argument can be applied to show that no one's action is free if God foreknows it. Both the premises seem initially plausible. It can't happen that God knows that something will be done when it won't. And if it *must be* that someone does a certain thing, if it *has* to happen, the action isn't free but forced. Moreover, the conclusion seems to follow straightforwardly from the premisses. So it looks like a sound argument for the incompatibility of divine foreknowledge and free human action.

One Response to the Argument

Boethius thought this was a sound argument (not surprisingly, given that it is his argument). His response was to accept the conclusion – God's foreknowledge really is incompatible with human free action – but to deny that God has foreknowledge. According to Boethius, God's special mode of existence is that of eternity, which he defines as "the complete possession all at once of illimitable life" (Boethius, 1962, Book 5, prose 6). From his eternal perspective, God sees everything that ever happens, all at once. God is thus "outside of time." This view of God's relation to time was dominant throughout much of subsequent history, and it received a popular endorsement in the 20th century by C. S. Lewis. Lewis wrote

> Everyone who believes in God at all believes that He knows what you and I are going to do tomorrow. But if he knows that I am going to do so and so, how can I be free to do otherwise? Well, here, once again, the difficulty comes from thinking that God is progressing along the Time line like us: the only difference being that He can see ahead and we cannot. Well, if that were true, if God foresaw our acts, it would be very hard to understand how we could be free not to do them. But suppose God is outside and above the Time line. In that case, what we call "tomorrow" is visible to Him in just the same way as what we call "today." All the days are "Now" for Him. (Lewis, 1953, p. 133)

So Lewis joins Boethius in thinking that we can avoid the apparent incompatibility of divine foreknowledge and human free action by holding that God is outside of time, that he has his knowledge from his eternal, atemporal perspective.

Regardless of whether God is most appropriately thought of as eternal or as everlasting in time, appealing to divine eternity does not help settle the question of whether divine omniscience is compatible with free action. The reason is that an exactly analogous argument can be given to argue that divine *eternal* knowledge is incompatible with human free action; so appealing to divine eternity does not by itself resolve the issue.[3] Consider,

> (1*)   If God has eternal knowledge that S does A at t, then S must necessarily do A at t.
> (2*)   If S must necessarily do A at t, then S doesn't do A freely at t.
> ∴ (3*)   If God has eternal knowledge that S does A at t, then S doesn't do A freely at t.

If the original argument shows that divine foreknowledge is incompatible with human free action, this argument does the same for divine eternal knowledge. So there seems to be no alternative but to look more closely at the original argument.

A Better Response to the Argument

Let's take a closer look at the premisses of the argument,

> (1)   If God foreknows that S will do A, then S must necessarily do A.
> (2)   If S must necessarily do A, then S will not do A freely.

Boethius' phrase "must necessarily" emphatically (or redundantly) attributes necessity to something or other, but to what? It's easy enough to say in the case of (2), which is naturally read as

> (2')   If it is necessary that S will do A, then S will not do A freely.

But with (1) we have a choice. It can be read in a couple of ways, like the slogan on a poster during World War II

> Save soap and waste paper!

Or the similarly ambiguous

Standing on the balcony he watched the fireworks go off in his slippers.

One thing that might be said to be necessary in (1) is a certain conditional; thus

(1') It is necessary that if God foreknows that *S* will do *A*, then *S* will do *A*.

Another interpretation is that, according to (1), if its antecedent is true, its consequent is necessary, that is,

(1") If God foreknows that *S* will do *A*, then the proposition that *S* will do *A* is necessarily true.[4]

Making this distinction gives us two arguments to evaluate, one with (1') as its first premise and the other with (1"). Let's represent the two arguments schematically. To do so, we will let "□" represent the necessity operator ("it is necessary that"), and we can use letters to abbreviate the various propositions:

K = God foreknows that *S* will do *A*.
D = *S* does *A*.
not-F = *S* will not do *A* freely.

The two arguments, then, are

I.	(1')	□(If K then D).	II.	(1")	If K then □D.
	(2')	If □D then not-F.		(2')	If □D then not-F.
∴	(3')	If K then not-F.	∴	(3')	If K then not-F.

Let's start with Argument I. Its first premiss, (1'), is clearly true. It expresses the necessary connection between knowledge and truth – necessarily anything *known* to be true *is* true. But this argument is invalid. To show this we'll use the strategy we stated in the first chapter and employed in our evaluation of Aquinas' Third Way; namely, we'll exhibit another argument of the same form with true premises and a false conclusion. That will show that it's possible for an argument of this form to have true premises and a false conclusion, and that means that arguments of that form are invalid. Consider your friend Matthew, currently a bachelor but regarded by some as a good catch. Whatever you think of Matthew's prospects of finding that special person, it is surely possible that he marry someone. In fact, for many of the people you know or know of, there are possible worlds where Matthew is married to one of them. Now let's assign a different interpretation to the sentence letters. That will give us another argument of the same form. This time

K = Matthew is a bachelor.
D = Matthew is unmarried.
not-F = There is no possible world in which Matthew has a spouse.

Under this interpretation, (1') is true. It's necessary that if Matthew is a bachelor then he is unmarried. And (2') is also true. If it is necessary that Matthew is a bachelor, there is no possible world where he has a spouse. But the conclusion, (3'), is false. If Matthew is a bachelor, it follows that he doesn't in fact have a spouse, not that it is not even possible for him to have one. So Argument I is invalid.

Turn now to Argument II. It has the virtue of being valid. It is of this form: if *p* then *q*; if *q* then *r*; therefore, if *p* then *r*; and this form is clearly valid. But (1″) is false. If God knows a proposition to be true, it doesn't in general follow that the proposition is a necessary truth, like *All triangles have three sides*. There are many contingent truths that you and I know. God knows them, too. So he can know a proposition without it being necessary.

There are thus two interpretations of the argument suggested by Boethius. Under the first, the argument has all true premises, but it is invalid. Under the second interpretation the argument is valid, but the first premiss is false. Both interpretations are therefore defective. This argument doesn't show the incompatibility of divine foreknowledge and human free action.

A Harder Objection

A much more difficult argument for the incompatibility of divine fore-knowledge, or more carefully, divine prior beliefs about the future,[5] and free human action appeals to the fact that the past is apparently fixed or settled. We saw in the last chapter that Anselm, for example, held that not even omnipotence includes the ability "to undo what has been done" (Anselm of Canterbury, 1998, *Proslogion*, 7). When something is "over and done with" it can no longer be affected. William of Ockham (1288–1347) used the term *accidental necessity* to designate the way in which contingent propositions can become fixed by being past.[6] Perhaps you have never visited Paris, but you do have a choice about whether to go there. In that case, the proposition that you have never visited Paris is true but it is not accidentally necessary. There is something you can do, namely, visit Paris, that would make it false. On the other hand, if you actually visit the City of Light, it will then be forever fixed or settled or accidentally necessary that you *have* visited Paris. After your visit, there will be nothing that you or anyone can do that will make it true that you have never been to Paris.

We can state the harder argument in terms of this concept of accidental necessity. The argument requires three principles about accidental necessity:

(4) True contingent propositions reporting God's past beliefs are forever after accidentally necessary.

If God had a certain belief a long time ago, that is something about the past that is now accidentally necessary.

(5) A contingent proposition entailed by an accidentally necessary proposition is itself accidentally necessary.

If a proposition is accidentally necessary at a certain time and it couldn't be true without some other contingent proposition being true, then that second proposition is then accidentally necessary, too.

(6) If a proposition is accidentally necessary at a time, then no one is able at any later time to make it false.

(6) is just what you would expect, if accidental necessity captures the fixity of the past.

Now suppose, to take an example introduced into the literature by Nelson Pike (1965), that it is true that

(7) Eighty years ago God believed that Jones will mow his lawn tomorrow.

Since this is a contingently true proposition reporting a past belief of God's, by (4), it is accidentally necessary, that is,

(8) It is accidentally necessary that eighty years ago God believed that Jones will mow his lawn tomorrow.

At this point the argument needs a slightly stronger assumption than that God is omniscient. It requires the assumption either that God is *essentially omniscient* (it's not possible that he exist without being omniscient) or that he is *infallible* (it is not possible that he believe a proposition and that proposition be false). Since the theist typically accepts both of these claims, let us grant them.[7] Given this assumption, it follows that the proposition that 80 years ago God believed that Jones will mow his lawn tomorrow *entails* that Jones will mow his lawn tomorrow. So by (5), the principle that accidental necessity is closed under (contingent) entailment, it follows from (8) that

(9)   It is accidentally necessary that Jones will mow his lawn tomorrow.

But from (6) and (9) it follows that there is nothing anyone can do to make

(10)   Jones will mow his lawn tomorrow

false. In particular, there is nothing Jones himself can do to make (10) false. So, if 80 years ago God believed that Jones will mow his lawn tomorrow, mowing his lawn tomorrow is a chore Jones is *unable* to shirk, that is,

(11)   Jones is not free with respect to mowing his lawn tomorrow.

This argument may, of course, be generalized to cover any human action about which God has had the prior belief that it would be done.

Replies to the Argument

If you want to avoid accepting the conclusion, there are, from a logical point of view, four options: you could deny one of the three principles about accidental necessity, (4), (5), or (6), or you could deny the assumption, (7), that God had a belief in the past about Jones' future mowing.

Those who hold that God is eternal or outside of time will deny (7). But that doesn't completely let them off the hook; for, just as in the case of our earlier argument, this one can be modified to apply to eternal knowledge. Simply revise (7) to

(7')   Eighty years ago it was then true that God had the eternal belief that Jones will mow his lawn tomorrow.

This replaces the alleged past truth about what God earlier believed with one about what was earlier true about God's atemporal beliefs. The rest of the argument can remain the same.[8] So endorsing divine eternity will not by itself resolve the difficulty posed by this argument. In any event, to deny (7) is, in effect, to give up the assumption that God has beliefs about free actions in our future.[9] Since our project is to examine whether divine foreknowledge is incompatible with human free action, let's consider other possible replies to the argument. We'll take up the three principles (4), (5), and (6) in reverse order.

One might be tempted to deny

(6)　If a proposition is accidentally necessary at a time, then no one is able at any later time to make it false.

Alvin Plantinga, for example, has suggested that even if

(7)　Eighty years ago God believed that Jones will mow his lawn tomorrow

is true and, hence, accidentally necessary, there might nevertheless be something that Jones is able to do, namely, refraining from mowing his lawn, which is such that, if he were to do it, then God wouldn't have believed 80 years ago that Jones will mow his lawn tomorrow. Instead, he would have believed that Jones will refrain from mowing his lawn tomorrow. On this suggestion, Jones is able to do something which is such that if he did it, (7) would have been false, and, hence, not accidentally necessary (Plantinga, 1986). This sort of "counterfactual power" over the past, however, is controversial. Moreover, it's not clear why someone who holds that both (7) and

(10)　Jones will mow his lawn tomorrow

are accidentally necessary should concede that Jones nevertheless has it within his power to refrain from mowing the lawn tomorrow. If we have any grasp at all of accidental necessity, shouldn't we think that what is now accidentally necessary is not within our power to circumvent? At any rate, I won't attempt to defend this solution to the argument.

Let's turn then to

(5)　A contingent proposition entailed by an accidentally necessary proposition is itself accidentally necessary.

The 16th-century Iberian philosopher Luis de Molina (1535–1600) apparently denied (5) (Molina, 1988, Disputation 52, section 34; see also Freddoso's discussion in his introduction to this volume, pp. 55–62). But, to the extent that we understand accidental necessity, (5) seems to be an obvious truth. There is, in fact, a simple argument for (5) that appeals to two even more evident claims. First,

(12)   Any proposition that is logically equivalent to an accidentally necessary proposition is itself accidentally necessary.

If a proposition p is fixed and unalterable in virtue of what has happened, if there is therefore nothing anyone can do to render p false, then how could there be another proposition, q, which is logically equivalent to p – true in exactly the same possible circumstances in which p is – which is not similarly fixed and inevitable? Second,

(13)   Any conjunction that has as a conjunct a contingent proposition that is not accidentally necessary is itself not accidentally necessary.

Suppose that p is not accidentally necessary and that there is something you could do that would make it false. If you were to do that and make p false, then for any proposition, q, the conjunction of p & q would also be false. So the truth of the conjunction is not something that is fixed or unalterable.

With the help of (12) and (13) we can construct an argument for (5). Let p be any proposition that is now accidentally necessary, and suppose that p entails some contingent proposition, q. Since p entails q, it is logically equivalent to the conjunction p & q.[10] By (12) this conjunction is accidentally necessary. But if this conjunction is accidentally necessary, then, by (13), it does not have any (contingent) conjuncts that are not accidentally necessary. By assumption, q is a contingent conjunct of p & q, so q is accidentally necessary. Hence, if p is accidentally necessary and entails a contingent proposition, q, q is also accidentally necessary. But this is just what (5) asserts.[11]

That leaves us with

(4)   True contingent propositions reporting God's past beliefs are forever after accidentally necessary

to consider. According to William of Ockham, some propositions that are apparently about the past are not *strictly* about the past, and only propositions that are strictly about the past are accidentally necessary. He wrote,

> Some propositions are about the present as regards both their wording and their subject matter. Where such [propositions] are concerned, it is universally true that every true proposition has [corresponding to it] a necessary one about the past – e.g., "Socrates is seated," "Socrates is walking," "Socrates is just," and the like.
>
> Other propositions are about the present as regards their wording only and are equivalently about the future, since their truth depends on the truth of propositions about the future. Where such [propositions] are concerned, the rule that every true proposition about the present has [corresponding to it] a necessary one about the past is not true. (William of Ockham, 1983, pp. 46–47)

On Ockham's view, a proposition like *Jones is walking his dog* is strictly about the present, and there is thus a corresponding accidentally necessary proposition about the past, for example, *A week ago it was true that Jones will walk his dog*. Given that Jones is now walking his dog, it is settled or fixed this *was* going to be the case. But *Jones will mow his lawn tomorrow* is partly about the future, and so the corresponding proposition, *A week ago it was true that Jones will mow his lawn tomorrow*, is not now accidentally necessary.

Similarly, some propositions are strictly about the past, for example, *Last week Smith believed that Jones will mow his lawn tomorrow*. But other propositions are about the past "as regards their wording only and are equivalently about the future." An example is *Last week Smith correctly believed that Jones will mow his lawn tomorrow*; this proposition depends for its truth (if it is true) on the future turning out a certain way. In more recent terms, *Last week Smith believed that Jones will mow his lawn tomorrow* reports a *hard* fact about the past, whereas *Last week Smith correctly believed that Jones will mow his lawn tomorrow* reports a *soft* fact about the past.[12] An Ockhamist reply to our argument, then, has two parts. The first is to claim that only propositions reporting hard facts about the past are now accidentally necessary – propositions reporting soft facts about the past are not accidentally necessary because they depend on the future, which is not yet settled, turning out in a particular way. The second is to claim that true propositions describing God's past beliefs about the contingent future are not accidentally necessary because they depend, in part, on the future turning out a certain way; accordingly, they report soft facts about the past. Thus, the Ockhamist provides an objection to the premiss

(4)   True contingent propositions reporting God's past beliefs are forever after accidentally necessary.

Propositions describing God's past beliefs, if they are not strictly about the past or if they report soft facts about the past, need not be accidentally necessary. If this is right, the harder argument for the incompatibility of divine foreknowledge and human free action has a false premiss and is, thus, also a failure.

Notes

1   Officially our position will be that defining omniscience is simple, but questions can be raised about whether there are restrictions on the range of true propositions. We'll consider below some issues about knowledge of propositions about the future. For additional complications see Wierenga (1989), chapters 2–6 and Wierenga (2009), pp. 129–144.

2   If it is possible for someone to know all true propositions while at the same time believing a falsehood, we should add to the definition either that an omniscient being believes no falsehoods or that the beliefs of an omniscient being are logically consistent.

3   Several authors have made this point, including Alvin Plantinga (1986), pp. 235–269, Wierenga (1989), p. 63, and Zagzebski (1985).

4   Although some philosophers have been taken in by Boethius' argument, the distinction just drawn and its bearing on this form of argument was noted already by Aquinas (1948 [1485], *Summa Theologiae*, I, 14, 13, *ad* 3).

5   I'll state the argument in terms of God's prior beliefs rather than in terms of his foreknowledge to forestall an objection to premiss (4). Some people might deny that God's past foreknowledge of a proposition is always accidentally necessary because, if it's really knowledge, it entails that the proposition will be true in the future. But a past belief, considered simply as a certain mental state, doesn't typically have such implications about the future. We'll see, in the end, that this maneuver isn't really necessary.

6   Ockham's use of this term apparently derives from the 13th-century logician, William of Sherwood. Because propositions that are accidentally necessary acquire that status as time goes by (and they might not have), they are not logically or metaphysically necessary – a status that doesn't change over time. This is why principles (4) and (5) below are restricted to *contingent* propositions.

7   Or assume their disjunction, if you want to minimize assumptions. Given this assumption, *God believes p* entails *p*; so switching from God's foreknowledge to God's forebelief (see note 4) does not really make a difference.

8   That the argument can be restated simply in terms of past truth (rather than past beliefs of God), suggests the following fatalistic argument:

   (7*)   Eighty years ago it was true that Jones will mow his lawn tomorrow. (assumption)

∴ (8*) It is accidentally necessary that eighty years ago it was true that Jones will mow his lawn tomorrow. (7*) and the analogue of (4), that truths about the past are accidentally necessary.

∴ (9*) It is accidentally necessary that Jones will mow his lawn tomorrow. (8*) and the assumption that *Eighty years ago it was true that Jones will mow his lawn tomorrow* entails *Jones will mow his lawn tomorrow*.

∴ (10*) There is nothing anyone can do to make it false that Jones will mow his lawn tomorrow. (9*), (6)

∴ (11) Jones is not free with respect to mowing his lawn tomorrow.

This argument can, of course, be generalized. Thus, it purports to show that if it is true ahead of time that someone will perform an action, the person isn't free with respect to that action. Some philosophers are willing to deny that there are any truths about future free actions. See, for example, Geach (1977) or the so-called "open theists," including the contributors to Pinnock *et al.* (1994). But if I tell you that I will (freely) do something I can legitimately complain if you don't believe me, and it isn't a good defense for you to claim that it wouldn't be rational for you to believe a proposition that wasn't yet true. At any rate, denying that there are truths about the contingent future, including future free actions, is an extreme position that should only be taken if there were a compelling reason for it. If the argument above were sound, that might be such a reason. It is thus a matter of some importance to examine whether any of the principles (4), (5), and (6) are questionable, or whether we really are better off denying the assumption (7*). In any event, I hope that noticing the parallel between this argument for fatalism and the argument we are considering in the text will incline you to think that the project of examining (4), (5), and (6) is a legitimate endeavor and not merely a desperate move to avoid concluding that divine foreknowledge is incompatible with our free action. After all, in order to avoid accepting the parallel argument for fatalism, one will need to find a reason to reject (the analogue of) (4), (5), or (6).

9   William P. Alston denies that God has beliefs (although he has knowledge), but this is a minority opinion. See his "Does God Have Beliefs?" (Alston, 1987).

10 If p entails q, then in every possible world in which p is true, q is also true. So every world in which p is true is a world in which p & q is true. And, of course, every world in which p & q is true is a world in which p is true. So if p entails q, p and p & q are true in exactly the same possible worlds and are thus logically equivalent.

11 This is a version of an argument I presented in Wierenga (1991), see pp. 428–429.

12 The terms "hard fact" and "soft fact" were introduced by Nelson Pike in "Of God and Freedom: A Rejoinder" (Pike, 1966). It is not a simple task to make this distinction precise. For a collection of papers on the topic, see Fisher (1989).

Suggested Reading

Thomas Flint, *Divine Providence: The Molinist Account* (Ithaca, NY: Cornell University Press, 1998).

Edward Wierenga, "Omniscience," in Thomas Flint and Michael Rea, eds, *Oxford Handbook of Philosophical Theology* (Oxford: Oxford University Press, 2009), pp. 129–144.

Linda Zagzebski, *The Dilemma of Freedom and Foreknowledge* (New York: Oxford University Press, 1991).

8

Divine Freedom and Moral Perfection

The Compossibility of the Divine Attributes?

We considered in Chapter 6 an objection to the divine attribute of omnipotence which claimed that omnipotence was incoherent or impossible for anyone to have. In Chapter 7 we considered a different objection to another divine attribute, namely, the contention that divine omniscience (given that it includes foreknowledge) is incompatible with something most of us accept: that we often act with free will. In this chapter we turn to a third sort of objection to the divine attributes – not that one or another is incoherent or that possessing them is incompatible with some widely accepted truth. Rather, this type of objection alleges that certain of the divine attributes are *incompatible with each other*, so no being could have all of them. Versions of this objection have targeted various divine attributes. Some philosophers think that omniscience is incompatible with omnipotence, holding that some kinds of knowledge require experiences that are not available to an omnipotent being (see Blumenfeld, 1978). Others might think that omnipotence is incompatible with impeccability (being unable to sin), maintaining that omnipotence includes all abilities, including the ability to sin.[1] There has also been a lively dispute about whether divine omniscience is compatible with divine immutability. Traditionally theists have held that God cannot change in any way, but some philosophers claim that omniscience requires knowing different things at different times, and a change in knowledge is a kind of change.[2]

I propose to discuss a different challenge to the compossibility of the divine attributes, the claim that perfect goodness is incompatible with divine freedom. I keep appealing to Richard Swinburne's characterization

The Philosophy of Religion, First Edition. Edward R. Wierenga.
© 2016 Edward R. Wierenga. Published 2016 by John Wiley & Sons, Ltd.

of theism as the claim that there is someone "without a body (i.e. a spirit) who is eternal, free, able to do anything, knows everything, is perfectly good, is the proper object of human worship and obedience, the creator and sustainer of the universe" (Swinburne, 1993, p. 1). Both *being free* and *being perfectly good* appear on this list. Theism would thus be impossible if freedom and perfect goodness were incompatible with each other.

Is There a Best Possible World?

William Rowe has developed some forceful arguments for the claim that divine freedom and perfect goodness are incompatible with each other.[3] His objection begins by asking whether there is a best of all possible worlds. Gottfried Wilhelm Leibniz famously held that the actual world is the best of all possible worlds. In his *Theodicy* Leibniz imagines a character, Theodorus, the High Priest, who dreamed that he was given a tour of a palace by the goddess, Pallas. Pallas led Theodorus into a hall of the palace, but when he entered it, it was no longer a hall but a world. A great volume of writings in the hall gave a complete description of everything that happened in that world. They visited another hall – another world – in which individuals similar to those in the first world did different things and led different lives. They visited more halls, and

> The halls rose in a pyramid, becoming even more beautiful as one mounted towards the apex, and representing more beautiful worlds. Finally they reached the highest one which completed the pyramid, and which was the most beautiful of all: for the pyramid had a beginning, but one could not see its end; it had an apex, but no base; it went on increasing to infinity. That is (as the Goddess explained) because amongst an endless number of possible worlds there is the best of all, else would God not have determined to create any; but there is not any one which has not also less perfect worlds below it: that is why the pyramid goes on descending to infinity. Theodorus, entering this highest hall, became entranced in ecstasy; he had to receive succor from the Goddess, a drop of a divine liquid placed on his tongue restored him; he was beside himself for joy. We are in the real true world (said the Goddess) and you are at the source of happiness. (Leibniz, 1985, para. 415)

The story is fanciful, but Leibniz is serious about what it represents. The volumes that Theodorus finds in each hall (world) provide a complete description of the history and the future of that world.[4] The various possible worlds correspond to complete ways things could go. (Recall our discussion in Chapter 5.) One way things could go is the way they really are going. In this world Theodorus sees Sextus scorning the counsel of the gods, violating his friend's wife, and making enemies. In another world Sextus obeys the gods, becomes king, and is adored by his subjects.[5] The other worlds are thus the other possible ways things could go. The vertical dimension of the pyramid represents Leibniz's assumption that worlds may be compared with respect to their greatness or intrinsic value. The closer to the top a world is, the better it is. In addition, there are infinitely many worlds, and every world has infinitely many worlds below it that are "less perfect" than it. But there is only one world at the top of the pyramid. There is one world uniquely better than all the other worlds; so there is a best of all possible worlds.

Of course, this picture is not an *argument* for the claim that there is a best possible world. Leibniz' reason for thinking that there is a best world drew on his commitment to the *Principle of Sufficient Reason*. According to this principle, there is a good reason for anything that happens; in particular, God has a good reason for anything that he does. Leibniz thought that God would have a good reason for making a world actual only if that world were better than any other world. Given that one world *is* actual, God must have had a reason for making it actual, and that could only be because it is the best.[6]

On the other hand, some philosophers have thought that God could have created a better world, and this at least suggests that there is no limit to how good a world can be. Aquinas, for example, holds that "God can do better than what he does." As Aquinas sees it, there are two things that contribute to the greatness of a world: its order and its parts (or the kinds of things that it contains). He says,

> Given the things which actually exist, the universe cannot be better, for the order which God has established in things, and in which the good of the universe consists, most befits things. For if any one thing were bettered, the proportion of order would be destroyed; just as if one string were stretched more than it ought to be, the melody of the harp would be destroyed. Yet God *could make other things*, or *add something* to present creation; and then there would be another and a better universe. (Aquinas, 1948 [1485], *Summa Theologiae* Ia., 25, 6, *ad* 3 (emphasis added). [7]

So by making different things or by adding more things to this world, God could have made a better world. It's not obvious that this commits Aquinas to the claim that the world could be improved *without limit* or that there is no best possible world. But Richard Swinburne has a suggestion that could help Aquinas to this conclusion. He writes,

> ...for any world of conscious agents which God could create *ex nihilo*, there is plausibly a better one – for instance, one obtained by adding one more conscious agent (sufficiently distant from the others not to crowd them). And so among the actions of creating conscious agents *ex nihilo* there is no best. What goes for conscious agents goes also for creating inanimate things *ex nihilo*. And no doubt ... for much else, too, for the kinds of knowledge and powers he gives to things and for the length of days he keeps them in being. (Swinburne, 1994, p. 135)

More generally, if whatever it is that contributes to the value of a world are things that can be increased without limit – whether these are conscious agents, or conscious agents living virtuous lives, or sentient beings experiencing pleasure, etc. – then, since there is no limit to how much of these things a world can contain, there is no limit to how good a world can be.

We do not have to settle the question of whether there is a best possible world, however, for Rowe's objection to apply, for he holds that there is a problem in either case. Let's turn, then, to the details of the objection.

Perfect Goodness and Divine Freedom

Rowe claims, in the first place, that if there is a best of all possible worlds, God's perfections require that he create or actualize that one.[8] As Rowe puts it, "given that God exists and that there is a best creatable world, God's nature as an omnipotent, omniscient, perfectly good being would require him to create that best world. Doing less than the best he can do – create the best creatable world – would be inconsistent with his being the perfect being he is" (Rowe, 2002, p. 410). In this case, however, Rowe claims that God is not free. Rowe defends that claim in a preceding passage:

> On the assumption that God (the supremely perfect being) exists and that there is a best, creatable world, we've reached the conclusion that God is neither free not to create a world nor free to create a world less than the best creatable world. Indeed, God would of necessity create the best of the creatable worlds, leaving us with no basis for thanking him, or praising him for creating the world he does. (Rowe, 2002, p. 410)[9]

Rowe seems to be assuming an incompatibilist or libertarian account of free action (see Chapter 5) according to which you don't act freely if you have to do what you do or you can't avoid doing what you do. Thomas Flint puts the view like this: "an agent is truly free with respect to an action only if the situation in which he is placed is logically and causally compatible with both his performing and his not performing the action" (Flint, 1983, p. 255). On this view, then, if God is logically required to actualize a certain world, he doesn't do so freely.

What if there is no best of all possible worlds? What if for any world God can actualize there is a better world he could actualize instead? In that case, Rowe claims that God would not be perfectly good. Rowe endorses the following principle:

> (B)   If an omniscient being creates a world when there is a better world that it could have created, then it is possible that there exists a being morally better than it. (Rowe, 2002, p. 412)

If God is confronted with an infinite series of better and better worlds, then whichever one he actualizes, it would be possible for him to actualize a better world. In that case, according to (B), it would be possible for there to be someone morally better than God. But if it is possible for someone to be morally better than God, then God isn't perfectly good.

We can summarize Rowe's argument as follows:

> (1)   Either there is a best of all possible worlds or there is not.
> (2)   If there is a best of all possible worlds, then God is not free (since he would have to create that world).
> (3)   If there is no best of all possible worlds, then God is not perfectly good (since whichever one he creates, it is possible that he create a better one).
> ∴ (4)   Either God is not free or God is not perfectly good. (1) (2) (3)
> ∴ (5)   God is not both free and perfectly good. (4)

So whether or not there is a best of all possible worlds, God isn't both free and perfectly good. If this argument is sound, it's not possible that God be both free and perfectly good – these divine attributes are incompatible with each other.

Some Initial Objections to the Argument

I think that both (2) and (3) are dubious. I realize that my reasons for being skeptical of them might not persuade everyone, but if either of these initial objections is correct, we will have found a flaw in the argument. First let's consider

> (2)   If there is a best of all possible worlds, then God is not free (since he would have to create that world).

I think we can grant (subject to a qualification to be introduced below) that if there is a best of all possible worlds, God's perfect goodness would require him to actualize it.[10] But why exactly should we think that this would make him unfree? We might agree that you and I are not free with respect to performing an action that we are caused to perform, especially if the cause in question is something like the manipulation of our brains by a nefarious neurosurgeon, or if it traces back to antecedent conditions that obtained before we were even born. A salient factor in such cases is that the causes in question are *external* to us. But if God is constrained by his own nature to do something, the constraint is not anything external to him. C. S. Lewis put the point like this:

> Whatever human freedom means, Divine freedom cannot mean indeterminacy between alternatives and choice of one of them. Perfect goodness can never debate about the end to be attained, and perfect wisdom cannot debate about the means most suited to achieve it. The freedom of God consists in the fact that no cause other than Himself produces His acts, and no external obstacle impedes them – that His own goodness is the root from which they all grow, and His own omnipotence the air in which they all flower. (Lewis, 1962, p. 35)

Perhaps, in other words, a constraint imposed by God's own nature would leave him free. If this is right, (2) is false.

I also doubt, with somewhat more confidence, that

(3)   If there is no best of all possible worlds, then God is not perfectly good (since whichever one he creates, it is possible that he create a better one)

is true. As we saw, Rowe attempts to support (3) by appealing to his principle

(B)   If an omniscient being creates a world when there is a better world that it could have created, then it is possible that there exists a being morally better than it.

But why should we think that the value of the result of an action redounds precisely to the moral value of the agent? Suppose that God was confronted with an infinite series of better and better worlds and, realizing that it is better to actualize one of them rather than none of them, decided to actualize one of them. To object that he could be morally improved, when the same criticism could with equal justice be raised no matter which of those worlds he actualized, seems mistakenly to blame God for an unavoidable fact about the situation in which he found himself. In his discussion of divine goodness Richard Swinburne writes that "where there is a best *kind of action* even if no best *action of that kind*, God's perfect goodness will lead to his doing some action of that best kind; for here is a maximum that can be attained and so ... a perfectly good being will do it" (Swinburne, 1994, p. 135, emphasis added). Actualizing a world with certain good features – human beings on the whole enjoying good lives, sentient creatures experiencing pleasure, a glorious diversity of life forms, etc., and a balance of good over evil – might be the best kind of world God can actualize, even if there is no best world of that kind. Perhaps, then, God is perfectly good in actualizing *some* world of that best kind, even if there is no best of all possible worlds.[11] If so, (3) is false.

A Somewhat More Complicated (But Compelling) Objection to the Argument

Up to this point we have ignored an alternative that might expose a loophole in the argument. If the reasons given by Aquinas and Swinburne in favor of an infinite series of better worlds are not convincing, then, either there is a best possible world or there are several worlds tied for best. In other words, there might be several equally good worlds with none better. If this is the situation God faced, then his perfect goodness would not have required him to actualize any particular one of them, and thus he would have been free to actualize any of them.[12] To apply this point to the argument, we may note that if there are multiple worlds tied for best, then:

(3)   If there is no best of all possible worlds, then God is not perfectly good (since whichever one he creates, it is possible that he create a better one)

is false. If there is no best of all possible worlds (that is, no uniquely best) but God actualizes one of the worlds tied for best, then it's not possible that he create a better one. Even conceding Rowe's principle (B), then, it doesn't follow that he is not perfectly good.

Rowe is not satisfied with this rejoinder. In a footnote he writes, "Even though there being several creatable worlds than which there are none better appears to leave God *free* to create any one of these worlds, ... proponents of this view are still burdened with having to defend the rather implausible claim that the actual world with all its evil is a world than which it is logically impossible that there should be a better world than it" (Rowe, 2002, n. 43, p. 132f). In the first part of this remark Rowe seems to concede the point that the alternative of multiple worlds tied for best would leave God free to create one of them. The second part of his reply seems mistaken, however. Rowe's argument is designed to show that divine freedom and perfect goodness are incompatible with each other, that there is no possible world where God has both of these properties. If Rowe is correct in denying that the actual world isn't really as good a world as can be, then, given the rest of his assumptions, it would follow that God isn't free and perfectly good in the actual world.[13] But as long as there is *some* world that is equally as good as some others and better than all the rest, Rowe seems to allow that in such a world God is both free and perfectly good. In that case, divine freedom and perfect goodness are not logically incompatible with each other.

There is a second complication we have not yet mentioned. There is a difference between a world's being possible and its being creatable, that is, its being a world that God is able to actualize. We have already seen in Chapter 5 how it could happen that a world is possible yet God is not able to make it actual. There we asked what would it take for God to be able to make it the case that

(19)   Person S freely and rightly chooses to do action A in circumstances C.

And we noted that God would have to be able to create S with free will and with the ability to perform A, and God would have to be able to place S in circumstances C and have it be the case that in C it would be right for S to perform A. But it would also depend on whether S would freely perform A or freely refrain from performing A in those circumstances. If S would freely perform A in those circumstances, then God could easily arrange for S to freely choose A in C. But if S would freely refrain from performing A in those circumstances, then if God created S with free will and placed S in C, S would *not* freely do A, and so (19) would not be true. Now (19) is true in many possible worlds, but if the fact of the matter is that S would refrain from doing A in C if God were to create S and place S in C, God wouldn't be able to actualize any of those worlds. If he tried to actualize a world in which S freely performs A in C (by creating S, placing S in C, and leaving S free in C), he'd get a world in which S freely refrains from A in C instead. More generally, which possible worlds God is able to actualize depends on which (contingent) counterfactuals of freedom are true.[14] Let's call those possible worlds that it was within God's power to make actual, *feasible* worlds.[15]

Given the distinction between possible worlds and feasible worlds, we can imagine several scenarios. Perhaps there is a best of all possible worlds, but it is not feasible. God's goodness would not require him to actualize the best world if he wasn't able to do so. Perhaps there is more than one equally good feasible world with no better feasible worlds. Then whether there is no limit to how good a possible world could be, there could be a top of the charts of feasible worlds. I don't think we're in a position to know exactly which feasible worlds were available to God. It could, in fact, be the case that the actual world is among the tied-for-best feasible worlds. Notice that sensibly to think this you wouldn't be "burdened with having to defend the rather implausible claim that the actual world with all its evil is a world than which it is logically impossible that there should be a better world than it." There could well be possible worlds much better than this one, but none of them feasible. It is at least possible that if God were to make his contribution toward actualizing a better world, *W*, free creatures he creates would wreak enough havoc so that the resulting world would not be *W* but some other world less good than the actual world.

We are now in a position to give a different reason for why

(2)   If there is a best of all possible worlds, then God is not free (since he would have to create that world), and

(3)   If there is no best of all possible worlds, then God is not perfectly good (since whichever one he creates, it is possible that he create a better one)

might both be false. If there is a best possible world but it is not feasible, then, since God's nature doesn't require him to do what he is unable to do, it doesn't follow that God isn't free. In that case, (2) is false. If there is no best possible world but there are several feasible worlds tied for best, it doesn't follow that God fails to do something less good than he can do, and it doesn't follow that God isn't perfectly good. He could do the best that he can by actualizing one of those best feasible worlds. So, (3) is false.

Now you might wonder whether Rowe's argument could be resuscitated by recasting it in terms of feasible worlds. Won't Rowe's objection arise with respect to them? Let's try stating the objection that way. It will be easier to keep track of the relevant options if we complicate (1) slightly.

(1')   Either there is a best of all feasible worlds, there is an infinite series of better and better feasible worlds (with no best), or there are several feasible worlds tied for best.

(2')   If there is a best feasible world, then God is not free (since he would have to create that world).

(3')   If there is an infinite series of better and better feasible worlds (with no best), then God is not perfectly good (since whichever one he creates, it is possible that he create a better one).

(3.5)   If there are several feasible worlds tied for best, then either God is not free or God is not good.

∴   (4)   Either God is not free or God is not perfectly good. (1) (2) (3) (3.5)

∴   (5)   God is not both free and perfectly good. (4)

I think that we can concede that (1') is true, since it seems to exhaust the alternatives. I think that (2') and (3') are dubious, however, for reasons parallel to those given above as initial objections to the argument, but I won't bother to repeat them. I have framed (3.5) in a way to permit the conclusion to follow. It wouldn't make a difference to the argument which of the attributes of freedom and perfect goodness God is supposed to lack if there are several feasible worlds tied for best; and if he lacks one, he lacks one or the other. So (3.5) provides what is required in order to derive the conclusion. But there is absolutely no reason to accept it.[16] So this version of the argument is unsuccessful, as well. We have thus found no reason to think that divine freedom and perfect goodness are incompatible.

Notes

1   Compare Nelson Pike (1969), who holds that the person who happens to be God has the ability to sin but would lose the title "God" if he did sin. This view requires the questionable assumption that the being who is God isn't essentially God. Our treatment in Chapter 6 followed Augustine and Aquinas in assuming that God cannot sin but that this ability is not required for him to be omnipotent.

2   Recent discussion was sparked by Kretzmann (1966). For references to some of the literature thus generated and proposed solutions, see my *The Nature of God* (Wierenga, 1989), pp. 175–190, as well as Wierenga (2001).

3   See Rowe (1993, 2002 and 2004). I have criticized Rowe's book in Wierenga (2007).

4   Alvin Plantinga calls the set of propositions true in a world *W*, *the book on W*. See Plantinga (1974), p. 46.

5   Sextus here is Sextus Tarquinius, a son of the last king of Rome, Tarquin the Proud. According to Livy (2006, *Ab Urbe Condita*, 1:57–58), public outrage over Sextus' rape of Lucretia led to the expulsion of the king and the establishment of the Roman Republic. A complication: Leibniz thinks that in another world it is "another Sextus," that no one exists in more than one possible world. We will ignore that complication and assume that the same individual can exist in different worlds.

6 "...there is an infinitude of possible worlds among which God must needs have chosen the best, since he does nothing without acting in accordance with supreme reason" (Leibniz, 1985, para. 8).

7 For a discussion of Aquinas on creation, see Kretzmann (1991).

8 We'll see below that it is important to distinguish between creating and actualizing a world. According to classical theism, God creates the universe. He makes the (contingent) things that exist. (Compare the first line of the Apostles' Creed: "I believe in God, the Father almighty, creator of heaven and earth.") Since a possible world is an abstract object, it exists necessarily and, thus, no one creates or makes it. Rather, by creating the things that he does and giving them the features they have, God makes actual or *actualizes* a certain possible world. Rowe is familiar with this distinction but often talks of creating a possible world rather than actualizing it.

9 I'm not persuaded that God doesn't deserve thanks or praise for features he has of necessity. On the other hand, Daniel Howard-Snyder concludes that the practice of praising and thanking God is irrational if God is essentially unsurpassably good. See Howard-Snyder (2009).

10 For a dissenting view, see Adams (1972); reprinted in his *The Virtue of Faith and Other Essays in Philosophical Theology* (1987).

11 Some philosophers have claimed that on this view God "satisfices", that is, settles for the "good enough" rather than the optimal, which they take to be morally problematic. See, for example, Kraay (2013). Chris Tucker has introduced a useful distinction between satisficing, conceived of as *aiming at less than the best* and "motivated submaximization," which is choosing less than the best because of a "countervailing consideration." Tucker thinks that the latter can be morally acceptable. One of his examples is choosing to perform an action that produces less total good than an alternative for the reason that it is better for one's own family. Choosing to actualize a world that is less than best because there is no best but it is good to actualize some world is another case of justifiably doing less than the best because of a countervailing consideration. See Tucker (2015).

12 Rowe is aware of this alternative. In *Can God Be Free?* he mentions "the possibility that although there are a number of worlds equally good and none better – a view that appears to leave God free to select from among those equally good words the one he will create" (p. 6f.), but he says remarkably little about it.

13 We have already seen in Chapter 5 that Rowe doesn't think that God exists in the actual world. See Rowe (1979 and 1996). This is weaker than the claim we are discussing in this chapter, which entails that it is *not possible* that God exists.

14 I have proposed a sketch of the relevant counterfactual conditionals God takes into account in creating in Wierenga (2011b).

15 The term is due to Thomas Flint. See the splendid discussion in his *Divine Providence: The Molinist Account* (Flint, 1998), especially pp. 51–54.

16   This is perhaps too strong. Maybe there's a reason to accept (3.5), just not a *good* reason. Leibniz thought that if faced with only equally good choices, God would be unable to pick any of them. He wrote, "In absolutely indifferent things there is no choice and consequently no election or will, since choice must be founded on some reason or principle" (Leibniz, 2000, p. 22). But, if there were a set of equally good worlds and no better, that would give God an overriding reason (Swinburne's term) to actualize one of them, even if it didn't give him a reason to pick a specific one, and one should think that he could find a way to choose.

Suggested Reading

Daniel and Frances Howard-Snyder, "How an Unsurpassable Being Can Create a Surpassable World," *Faith and Philosophy* 11(2) (1994): 260–268.
William Rowe, "Can God Be Free?," *Faith and Philosophy* 19(4) (2002): 405–424.
Edward Wierenga, "The Freedom of God," *Faith and Philosophy* 19(4) (2002): 425–436.

9

Miracles

Occasionally a dramatic sports victory, an extraordinary coincidence, or the birth of a healthy baby are called miracles. But sports upsets, lost pets finding their way home, the chance meeting of a friend in an unlikely place, and even the birth of a baby are not what philosophers or theologians have had in mind when they discussed miracles. For a dramatic example of an event that really seems miraculous, we can turn to a remarkable incident recounted in the 18th chapter of the book of I Kings. Under the reign of King Ahab and his wife, the original Jezebel, the people of Israel had begun to worship a rival deity, Baal. Elijah, a prophet of God, proposed a test. In front of a crowd of witnesses, he and the prophets of Baal would each prepare an altar for animal sacrifice. Then they would in turn call on their preferred god to ignite the offering. As the prophets of Baal danced around their altar, with cries and self-flagellation to no effect, Elijah made fun of them. When it was his turn, Elijah constructed an altar of stones, adding wood for fuel, and laid a slaughtered bull on it. To make the test even more difficult, he repeatedly doused the altar with water. Then, the text continues,

> At the time of the offering of the oblation, the prophet Elijah came near and said, "O Lord, God of Abraham, Isaac, and Israel, let it be known this day that you are God in Israel, that I am your servant, and that I have done all these things at your bidding. Answer me, O Lord, answer me, so that this people may know that you, O Lord, are God, and that you have turned their hearts back." Then the fire of the Lord fell and consumed the burnt offering, the wood, the stones, and the dust, and even licked up the water that was in the trench. When all the people saw it, they fell on their faces and said, "The Lord indeed is God; the Lord indeed is God." (I Kings 18: 36–39, NRSV)

The Philosophy of Religion, First Edition. Edward R. Wierenga.
© 2016 Edward R. Wierenga. Published 2016 by John Wiley & Sons, Ltd.

This story dramatically illustrates many of the features that seem central to the concept of a miracle: a divine or supernatural intervention; an occurrence that is inexplicable by natural causes or by the operation of the laws of nature; an event that is astonishing or amazing, taken to be a sign of religious significance.

You might think that events like this one never happened, or, if they did long ago, they don't anymore. But even today many people pray for or hope for a miracle, and in some cases they come to believe that a miracle has occurred. In recent years, the Roman Catholic Church has canonized hundreds of people, which requires, in each case, evidence of miracles that can be attributed to the candidate for sainthood. To understand what is being claimed in such cases, it seems best to begin by trying to understand what a miracle is supposed to be.

A Question of Definition

Many of the classical theists noted the features I called attention to in the example of Elijah and the altar. Augustine wrote that "a miracle is something difficult, which seldom occurs, surpassing the faculty of nature, and going far beyond our hopes as to compel our astonishment."[1] And Thomas Aquinas said that "a miracle is so called as being full of wonder, in other words, as having a cause absolutely hidden from all. This cause is God. Therefore those things which God does outside of the causes which we know are called miracles" (Aquinas, 1948 [1485], *Summa Theologiae*, Ia, 105, 7).

These remarks suggest that we might define a miracle as follows:

(D1)   An event e is a miracle $=_{df}$ (i) e violates natural laws, and (ii) e is caused by God.[2]

Should we also build into the definition that miracles are astonishing, or that they are signs of religious significance? Miracles often do, by their marvelous nature, serve the purpose of convincing people to believe some religious claim or accept the authority of some religious figure. That was certainly an important result of Elijah's calling down fire from heaven. But if God were to alter things in some hidden way, perhaps by changing someone's heart or by deflecting an unknown threat, that would also seem to count as miraculous. So let's not add astonishment to the definition.

It will come as no surprise that many people, including even some theologians, think that it is somehow misguided or at least unsophisticated to believe that there could be miracles, taken in this way. For example, the German theologian Rudolph Bultmann (1884–1976) held that "It is impossible to use electric light and the wireless and to avail ourselves of modern medical and surgical discoveries, and at the same time to believe in the New Testament world of spirits and miracles. We may think we can manage it in our own lives, but to expect others to do so is to make the Christian faith unintelligible and unacceptable to the modern world" (Bultmann, 1961, p. 5). Some thinkers have wanted to jettison the idea of supernatural intervention while nevertheless admitting a modified concept of miracle. Thus, the liberal Protestant theologian Paul Tillich (1886–1965) wrote that "Miracles cannot be interpreted in terms of a supranatural interference in natural processes.... A genuine miracle is first of all an event which is astonishing, unusual, shaking, without contradicting the rational structure of reality. In the second place, it is an event which points to the mystery of being, expressing its relation to us in a definite way. In the third place, it is an occurrence which is received as a sign-event in an ecstatic experience" (Tillich, 1951, p. 117). It's not easy to say what "contradicting the rational structure of reality" is, or in which direction one points to "point to the mystery of being." But it is clear that Tillich does not think that there could be an intervention of God that violated the laws of nature. So he denies the existence of miracles as they are defined by (D1). He seems willing to accept a substitute, however – something remarkable that functions as a sign. Perhaps, then, he would propose the following alternative definition:

(D2) e is a miracle $=_{df}$ (i) e is unusual, and (ii) e is a sign of religious significance.

This definition concentrates on those features that I had said were typical of miracles without being defining of them, namely that they are a source of amazement and that they are taken as evidence for some religious claim.

In this respect, (D2) seems to capture what R. F. Holland (1965) has called the "contingency concept" of miracle. Holland describes a case in which a small boy on a railroad track does not notice the approaching train. His mother, who sees the train, is unable to reach the boy or to attract his attention; so she prays that her son will be spared. As it happens, the train does stop, inches from the boy, but for completely natural reasons: the engineer has suffered a stroke, and when his hand fell off the throttle, the automatic braking mechanism of the train stopped it at just that point. Holland holds that it would be appropriate for the mother to regard the train's stopping as a miracle and that she could properly thank

God for it. Although there was no special act of God, no violation of the laws of nature, Holland suggests that the event was unusual and could be taken to have religious significance.

It's not clear, however, why such an event should be taken to have religious significance. It doesn't seem as though it would be *evidence* for a religious claim unless it were more than a coincidence. The train's stopping short of the boy, however desirable it was, seems no more a miracle than an underdog sports team winning or running into a friend in a foreign city. In any event, it is clear, I think, that the traditional view of miracles is one according to which they are understood in the sense of (D1). That is the kind of miracle that defenders of miracles affirm, and it is what opponents of miracles mean to deny. So let us explore that concept further.

An Immediate Objection

If a miracle really is, as (D1) affirms, a violation of a law of nature, then it seems as though there is an obvious and immediate objection. What are laws of nature if not regularities (or statements of regularities) that hold without exception? But then there couldn't be anything that violated them. Any regularity that admitted exceptions would not be a real law of nature. So if there are laws of nature, there aren't any exceptions to them. It would not help, moreover, to say that there really aren't any laws of nature, because there would not be any miracles in that case, either. If, by definition, a miracle is a violation of a law of nature, there could not be any miracles if there were no laws.

We can put this objection in the form of an argument:

    (1)   A law of nature is a regularity that holds without exception.
    (2)   A miracle is an exception to a law of nature.
∴ (3)   If there are laws of nature, there are no miracles. (1) (2)
∴ (4)   If there are no laws of nature, there are no miracles. (2)
    (5)   Either there are laws of nature or there are no laws of nature.
∴ (6)   There are no miracles. (3) (4) (5)

This argument is clearly valid. The only question to ask is whether its premisses are true. Premiss (5) is an instance of a law of logic, and (2) is a straightforward consequence of the definition (D1). That leaves only premiss (1) to be examined.

Why should we think that laws of nature hold without exception? Is it really *impossible* that there should be a divine intervention into the natural world? Imagine a peach tree from which the peaches are falling. Certain laws of nature (together with facts about the peaches and their environment) describe the path each peach follows as it falls, unhindered, to the ground. Now if someone stands underneath the tree and catches the peaches before they hit the ground, there is a sense in which those laws have been "violated." They describe the trajectory of the peach from branch to ground if no one interferes with it; but in cases in which there is an intervention, the laws admit exceptions. Now this example is deficient in an obvious way, because the same causal laws that describe how peaches move when the only forces acting on them are gravity and wind also describe their path when the opposing force of a hand is applied to them. In this example, the catcher and the peach are each physical parts of the same system, each subject to the same laws. But now imagine that, instead of a human catcher, there is a supernatural intervention into the situation which prevents the peaches from reaching the ground. It seems plausible to think that the causal laws, which describe how physical objects act on each other, simply do not extend to supernatural action. In that case, we should say that (1) isn't true after all. What's true instead is

(1')   A law of nature is a regularity that holds except when there is supernatural intervention.

But with (1') replacing (1) in the argument, the conclusion (3) no longer follows.

It might seem that this move is purely arbitrary, designed solely to accommodate the possibility of miracles. But no less an opponent of miracles than J. L. Mackie says something similar. He writes:

If miracles are to serve their traditional function of giving spectacular support to religious claims – whether general theistic claims, or the authority of some specific religion or some particular sect or individual teacher – the concept must not be so weakened that anything at all unusual or remarkable counts as a miracle. We must keep in the definition the notion of a violation of natural law. But then, if it is to be even possible that a miracle should occur, we must modify the definition ... of a law of nature. What we want to do is to contrast the order of nature with a possible divine or supernatural intervention. The laws of nature, we must say, describe the ways in which the world – including, of course, human beings – works when left to itself, when not interfered with. A miracle occurs when the world is not left to itself, when something distinct from the natural order as a whole intrudes into it. (Mackie, 1982, pp. 19–20)

In the first part of this passage, Mackie weighs in in support of (D1), or something like it, as the proper definition of a miracle. Then he recommends construing natural laws, as in (1'), according to which they only apply when the world is not interfered with by something outside the natural order. Let's adopt these suggestions, conceding that miracles are not by definition impossible, and look instead to a further complication.

A Brief Refinement

For ease of exposition of the distinction I have just introduced, between the regular operation of natural laws and divine intervention or violation of a natural law, I have made it seem as though divine intervention is rare and that divine action has nothing to do with how things normally go. But that is not how many theists have conceived of this distinction. The medievals, for example, thought that not only did God *create* the world but that he *continuously conserves* it; that is, God's action is required at all times to sustain or keep the world in existence. So God's action in the world is constant rather than rare. And it is a short step from the claim that God sustains things *at* each moment to the conclusion that he is responsible for how things go *from moment to moment*. In the latter case, God would bear at least some responsibility for changes that occur over time, that is for what we have been thinking of as the regular operation of causal laws.

This is how Samuel Clarke (1675–1729) thought of the matter. He held that

> All things that are done in the world are done either immediately by God himself, or by created intelligent beings: matter being evidently not at all capable of any laws or powers whatsoever, any more than it is capable of intelligence.... So that all those things which we commonly say are the effects of the natural powers of matter and laws of motion, of gravitation, attractions, or the like, are indeed (if we speak strictly and properly) the effects of God's acting upon matter continually and every moment.... The course of nature, truly and properly speaking, is nothing else but the will of God, producing certain effects in a continued, regular, constant and uniform manner. (Clarke, 1716, XIV, 3, pp. 300–301)

Given this account of God's involvement in ordinary affairs, Clarke made an appropriate adjustment in how to understand a miracle. He wrote:

> But if the course of nature be meant only (as it truly signifies) the constant and uniform manner of Gods [sic] acting either immediately or mediately in preserving and continuing the order of the world, then, in that sense,

indeed, a miracle may be rightly defined to be an effect produced contrary
to the usual course or order of nature, by the unusual interposition of some
intelligent being superior to men.... (Clarke, 1716, XIV, 3, p. 302)

According to Clarke's view, then, natural laws describe the way God *usually* acts in sustaining the universe, and miracles violate natural law only in
the sense that they are departures from the way God usually acts. It's easy
to see how this view would reply to the argument we considered in the last
section for the conclusion that miracles are by definition impossible.
Clarke, too, would deny

(1) A law of nature is a regularity that holds without exception.

He would hold instead that laws of nature are regularities that hold whenever God acts in his customary way.

So whether the laws of nature describe how things go when there is no
supernatural intervention, or whether they describe how God usually acts,
there seems to be no reason in principle to think that miracles could not
occur. But even if they are not impossible, would it ever be reasonable to
think that a miracle has occurred? This is a topic to which we turn in the
next section.

Hume's Objection

One of the most forceful objections to miracles is due to David Hume. His
claim is not that miracles could not happen, but that it is never rational to
believe that one has occurred on the basis of testimonial evidence. This
claim is important because most people do not themselves witness miracles; if they have any reason to think that they have occurred, it is due to
oral or written reports, such as that in I Kings 18. So if Hume is correct,
most people would not be rational in believing a miracle to have occurred.

Hume does not base his objection on a general skepticism toward testimonial evidence. Indeed, he says that "we may observe that there is no
species of reasoning more common, more useful, and even necessary to
human life, than that which is derived from the testimony of men, and the
reports of eye-witnesses and spectators."[3]

Instead, he thinks that there are some special principles for appraising
the value of testimonial evidence. He writes,

There are many ... particulars ... which may diminish or destroy the force of
any argument, derived from human testimony.

Suppose, for instance, that the fact which the testimony endeavors to establish, partakes of the extraordinary and the marvelous; in that case the evidence, resulting from the testimony, admits of a diminution, greater or less, in proportion as the fact is more or less unusual.[4]

So the value of testimonial evidence in favor of a proposition is reduced if that proposition is unlikely. Hume then appeals to his understanding that miracles violate natural laws:

A miracle is a violation of the laws of nature; and as a firm and unalterable experience has established these laws, the proof against a miracle, from the very nature of the fact, is as entire as any argument from experience can possibly be imagined.... There must, therefore, be a uniform experience against every miraculous event, otherwise the event would not merit that appellation. And as a uniform experience amounts to a proof, there is here a direct and *full* proof, from the nature of the fact, against the existence of any miracle....[5]

Finally, Hume puts these various pieces together and concludes:

The plain consequence is (and it is a general maxim worthy of our attention), "That no testimony is sufficient to establish a miracle, unless the testimony be of such a kind, that its falsehood would be more miraculous, than the fact which it endeavors to establish ..."; When anyone tells me, that he saw a dead man restored to life, I immediately consider with myself, whether it be more probable, that this person should either deceive or be deceived, or that the fact, which he relates, should really have happened. I weigh the one miracle against the other; and according to the superiority, which I discover, I pronounce my decision, and always reject the greater miracle.[6]

We can formulate Hume's argument as follows:

   (1)   If a person S testifies that a proposition p is true, then it is rational to believe p on the basis of S's testimony only if it is more likely that p is true than it is that S is mistaken in so testifying.

∴ (2)   If a person S testifies that a miracle has occurred, then it is rational to believe that a miracle has occurred on the basis of S's testimony only if it is more likely that a miracle has occurred than it is that S is mistaken in so testifying. (1)

   (3)   That a miracle has occurred is as improbable as any empirical (based on experience) proposition can be.

   (4)   That a person is mistaken in testifying to an empirical proposition is an empirical proposition.

∴ (5) It is not the case that it is more likely that a miracle has occurred than it is that *S* is mistaken in so testifying. (3) (4)

∴ (6) If a person *S* testifies that a miracle has occurred, then it is not rational to believe that a miracle has occurred on the basis of *S*'s testimony. (2) (5)

Despite its apparent plausibility, I think that there are two flaws in this argument. In the first place, I think the general principle, (1), about the diminution of testimonial evidence is mistaken. Second, I think that premiss (3) is dubious. I'll take these up in turn.

A lottery

Suppose we conduct a small lottery. We fill an urn with 100 balls, consecutively numbered from 1 to 100, and we distribute tickets corresponding to each number. I'll reach into the urn, draw a ball, and announce the winner. At the time for the drawing, I grab a ball and announce

I've drawn ball number 7.

Now I think that in these circumstances it would be rational for you to believe me. If you are holding ticket number 7, you would be rational in thinking that you had won. If you are holding any other ticket, it would be rational for you to think that you had not won. Now let's compare two probabilities. First, the probability that ball number 7 would be drawn is easy, given that it is a fair lottery: it's 1/100.

But what is the probability that I am mistaken in testifying that I have drawn ball number 7? I used the phrase "mistaken in testifying" to cover the two possibilities that Hume mentions, namely, that I am myself deceived or that I am attempting to deceive you. That suggests a range of ways in which I could be mistaken in my testimony: I might have misread the number; I might have tried to say "seventeen" but accidentally said "seven"; I might have known that my best friend was holding ticket number 7 and I wanted my friend to win. You will no doubt be able to think of other ways in which I was mistaken. Take them into account and estimate the probability of

I am mistaken in testifying that I have drawn ball number 7.

I will accept any answer here. Suppose you say 1/10,000. Then we have a case in which the proposition to which I've testified is more likely to be true than it is that I am mistaken. So far, we are in accord with Hume's principle (1).

Now let us change the example. Since you said that the probability that I am mistaken in testifying that I have drawn ball number 7 is 1/10,000, I will change the example to a lottery with an urn containing 100,000 balls. Let's conduct the drawing as before. Again, I announce that I have drawn ball number 7. This time the probability that ball number 7 would be drawn is considerably lower; it is 1/100,000. What of the probability that I am mistaken in testifying that I have drawn ball number 7? It is exactly the same as it was before. Perhaps a larger number would have introduced a greater chance of misreading the ball, but I've drawn the same number. And surely the likelihood that I am mistaken does not increase just because there were more balls to draw from. Suppose I meet you on the steps of the university library and ask what book you have just checked out. You look at the cover and say, "*War and Peace*." You would not have been any less likely to be mistaken in your testimony if you had checked the book out of a small community library. The size of the library from which the book was taken does not affect the probability of your being mistaken when you tell me the title.

So we have a case in which

Prob(I have drawn ball number 7) = 1/100,000, and
Prob(I am mistaken in testifying that I have drawn ball number 7) = 1/10,000.

But it *is* rational for you to believe that I have drawn ball number 7, despite it being more likely that I am mistaken in testifying than that that was the ball I drew. So Hume's premiss (1), which says otherwise, is false.[7]

How likely are miracles?

According to the third premiss of Hume's argument, that a miracle has occurred is as unlikely as any empirical proposition can be. Why should we think that to be true? J. L. Mackie offers a reason: "[If an event is a miracle then it] must, by the miracle advocate's own admission, be contrary to a genuine, not merely a supposed, law of nature and *therefore* [emphasis added] be maximally improbable" (Mackie, 1982, p. 25). If laws of nature hold without exception, this would be right. But if such laws always hold except when there is divine intervention, as Mackie has conceded, it is considerably less clear that miracles are maximally improbable. According to his view, there could not be a naturally occurring exception to a law of nature. So, it is maximally improbable that there is a naturally occurring exception to a law of nature. But nothing follows about how likely it is that there is a *supernatural* exception to a law of nature. How likely is it that there is divine intervention in the world? Exactly as likely as it is that there are miracles. And how likely is that? It isn't obvious or evident that it's highly unlikely.[8] But then we seem to have no reason to think that Hume's premiss (3) is true.

Alternatively, if laws of nature describe how God usually acts, as Samuel Clarke held, then it's even easier to know what to say about (3). Clarke himself put it as follows:

> it cannot be denied, but that it is altogether as easy to alter the course of nature, as to preserve it; that is, that miracles, excepting only that they are more unusual, are in themselves and in the nature and reason of the thing, as credible in all respects, and as easy to be believed, as any of those we call natural effects. (Clarke, 1716, XIV, 3, p. 303)

Conclusion

We have discussed how to define a miracle, and we've seen how laws of nature need to be understood in order for miracles not to be impossible by definition. Then we considered a famous and influential argument suggested by David Hume for the conclusion that it's not rational to believe on testimonial grounds that a miracle has occurred. I argued that one of the premises of that argument is false and another is dubious, so we have not seen that it's irrational to believe in miracles.

Notes

1 Augustine, *De Utilitate Credendi*, XVI, quoted in Aquinas (1948 [1485]), *Summa Theologiae*, I, 105, 7, obj 1.
2 If we liked, we could extend the definition to include events caused by other supernatural agents.
3 David Hume (1975), "Of Miracles," Section X of *An Enquiry Concerning Human Understanding*.
4 David Hume, "Of Miracles," Section X of *An Enquiry Concerning Human Understanding*.
5 David Hume, "Of Miracles," Section X of *An Enquiry Concerning Human Understanding*. Since this passage occurs within the context of Hume's argument about testimonial evidence, I do not think that he intends to be giving a separate general argument against the occurrence of miracles. Rather, the

"proof ... against the occurrence of any miracle" is a measure of how vastly improbable he thinks miracles are.

6 David Hume, "Of Miracles," Section X of *An Enquiry concerning Human Understanding*.

7 Robert Hambourger employs a lottery example to refute what he identifies as Hume's Principle of Relative Likelihood. See Hambourger (1980).

8 Perhaps this is overstating the case. We have lots of reasons to think that the laws of nature according to which, say, bridges don't collapse, airplanes remain in the air, and people deprived of oxygen die, are usually (and maybe always) in force. But recognizing this still leaves it unknown how likely it is that God influences people's thoughts or even intervenes with cures. So I do think that it's not clear that Hume is right when he says that a miracle is as unlikely as can be.

Suggested Reading

David Hume, "Of Miracles," Section X, *An Enquiry concerning Human Understanding* (1777), in *Enquiries Concerning Human Understanding and Concerning the Principles of Morals*, 3rd edn, ed. L. A. Selby-Bigge and P. H. Nidditch (Oxford: Clarendon Press, 1975).

Richard Swinburne, ed., *Miracles* (New York: Macmillan, 1989).

Peter van Inwagen, "Of 'Of Miracles'," in his *The Possibility of Resurrection and Other Essays in Christian Apologetics* (Boulder, CO: Westview Press, 1998), pp. 89–103.

10

The Evidentialist Objection: Clifford and James

We have looked at several ways of trying to prove that God exists and found them unconvincing. We have also looked at the leading attempt to show that God doesn't exist, namely, the problem of evil, and we've found it similarly unconvincing. Then we considered challenges to several of the divine attributes and concluded that these objections didn't show that the divine attributes were impossible, incompatible with each other, or otherwise suspect. Finally, we looked at some arguments designed to show either that miracles could not occur or at least that it's not rational (on only testimonial evidence) to believe that they do, and we concluded that these arguments did not succeed.

Where does that leave us? We haven't been able to prove theism to be true, but we haven't been able to prove it false, either. Is it rational or reasonable to believe something that you can't prove? An influential position on this topic holds that it is never rational to believe something for which you don't have good evidence. According to a well-known story, the philosopher Bertrand Russell (1872–1970), who didn't believe in God, was asked what he would say if after his death he found himself in God's presence. Russell replied, "I'd say, 'Not enough evidence, God, not enough evidence!'"[1] Russell's response indicates that he thought that he had taken the correct attitude toward God's existence, given the evidence available to him.

Clifford and "The Ethics of Belief"

The importance of evidence for rational belief was at the heart of a famous dispute near the end of the 19th century between the British mathematician and essayist, W. K. Clifford (1845–1879), and the

The Philosophy of Religion, First Edition. Edward R. Wierenga.
© 2016 Edward R. Wierenga. Published 2016 by John Wiley & Sons, Ltd.

American pragmatist philosopher, William James (1842–1910). Clifford began his essay, "The Ethics of Belief," with an example of a ship owner.

> A shipowner was about to send to sea an emigrant ship. He knew that she was old, and not over-well built at the first; that she had seen many seas and climes, and often had needed repairs. Doubts had been suggested to him that possibly she was not seaworthy. These doubts preyed upon his mind and made him unhappy; he thought that perhaps he ought to have her thoroughly overhauled and refitted, even though this should put him to great expense. Before the ship sailed, however, he succeeded in overcoming these melancholy reflections. He said to himself that she had gone safely through so many voyages and weathered so many storms that it was idle to suppose she would not come safely home from this trip also. He would put his trust in Providence, which could hardly fail to protect all these unhappy families that were leaving their fatherland to seek for better times elsewhere. He would dismiss from his mind all ungenerous suspicions about the honesty of builders and contractors. In such ways he acquired a sincere and comfortable conviction that his vessel was thoroughly safe and seaworthy; he watched her departure with a light heart, and benevolent wishes for the success of the exiles in their strange new home that was to be; and he got his insurance money when she went down in midocean and told no tales. (Clifford, 1979, pp. 177–178)

Clifford's assessment of the owner is brutal:

> What shall we say of him? Surely this, that he was verily guilty of the death of those men. It is admitted that he did sincerely believe in the soundness of his ship; but the sincerity of his conviction can in no wise help him, because *he had no right to believe on such evidence as was before him.* (Clifford, 1979, p. 178, original emphasis)

Clifford then modified the example:

> Let us alter the case a little, and suppose that the ship was not unsound after all; that she made her voyage safely, and many others after it. Will that diminish the guilt of her owner? Not one jot. When an action is once done, it is right or wrong forever; no accidental failure of its good or evil fruits can possibly alter that. The man would not have been innocent, he would only have been not found out. The question of right or wrong has to do with … whether he had a right to believe on such evidence as was before him. (Clifford, 1979, p. 178)

Whether the ship sailed safely or not, the ship owner's belief was wrong, according to Clifford, because the ship owner did not have sufficient evidence to support it.

Several aspects of Clifford's position are puzzling and require more exegesis than we can give them here. What does he mean by saying that a belief is wrong? What exactly makes a belief wrong? His condemnation is clear, however:

> If the belief has been accepted on insufficient evidence, the pleasure is a stolen one. Not only does it deceive ourselves by giving us a sense of power which we do not really possess, but it is sinful, because it is stolen in defiance of our duty to mankind. That duty is to guard ourselves from such beliefs as from a pestilence, which may shortly master our own body and spread to the rest of the town. (Clifford, 1979, p. 184)

The terms "stolen," "sinful," and "duty" suggest that Clifford thinks that it is *morally* wrong to accept a belief on insufficient evidence. Perhaps this is what he thinks, but I propose, in order to have a statement of the sort of view presupposed by Bertrand Russell, that we interpret the failure as intellectual or epistemic. More exactly, let's interpret Clifford as holding that a belief for which one doesn't have enough evidence is *irrational.*

We will also disregard two additional complications. In the case of the shipowner, the owner *ignores* some relevant evidence ("the ship is old," "the ship wasn't well-built in the first place," etc.) And in a different example later in the essay, Clifford has the offender holding a belief without having bothered to consider some easily available counter-evidence. Both of these topics raise interesting issues. But they are not relevant to Clifford's famous summary of his view:

> To sum up: it is wrong always, everywhere, and for anyone, to believe anything upon insufficient evidence. (Clifford, 1979, p. 186)

If we adopt the interpretation that "wrong" here means *irrational*, we can put Clifford's principle as

(1) It's rational to believe a proposition *p* only if there is sufficient evidence in favor of *p*.

(1) seems initially plausible. In fact, it might just be a way of spelling out Hume's sensible-sounding claim that "a wise man ... proportions his

belief to the evidence."[2] But it is easy to use (1) to construct an argument against the rationality of belief in God: simply add an additional premiss and then deduce the obvious conclusion:

> (2)   There isn't sufficient evidence in favor of the proposition that God exists.
> ∴   (3)   It's not rational to believe that God exists. (1) (2)

James and "The Will to Believe"

William James began an address to the philosophical clubs of Yale and Brown by saying that:

> I have brought with me to-night something like a sermon on justification by faith to read to you, – I mean an essay in justification *of* faith, a defense of our right to adopt a believing attitude in religious matters, in spite of the fact that our merely logical intellect may not have been coerced. (James, 1897, pp. 1–2)

If our "logical intellect" isn't "coerced" into believing something, that is presumably because the evidence for it isn't strong or forceful enough. James thus aims to counter Clifford's claim that it is *always* wrong to believe something without sufficient evidence. He attempts this by delineating one very specific kind of case in which he thinks it is permissible or rational to believe something without good evidence, and he claims that this applies to the case of religious belief.

James's central thesis in this reply to Clifford – his "doctrine of the will to believe" – employs a technical term that he introduces by way of a series of definitions. In order to grasp that thesis, we will first have to wade through those definitions.

First, a *hypothesis* is "anything that may be proposed for belief." Given that the objects of beliefs are *propositions*, hypotheses, then, are propositions, ones that someone offers for belief. A hypothesis may be either *live* or *dead*. A live hypothesis is "one that appeals as a real possibility" to the person to whom it is proposed. A dead hypothesis has no such appeal. Whether a hypothesis is live or dead is thus relative to individual persons, since a proposition can have some appeal to one person but not to another. Next, an *option* is a decision between two hypotheses. An option is *living* if both hypotheses are live, and it is *dead* if at least one of the hypotheses is dead. An option is *forced* if you have to pick one of the hypotheses, and it is *avoidable* if you can avoid choosing. James illustrates this distinction as follows:

> If I say to you: "Choose between going out with your umbrella or without it," I do not offer you a [forced] option. You can easily avoid it by not going out at all. Similarly, if I say, "Either love me or hate me," "Either call my theory true or call it false," your option is avoidable. You may remain indifferent to me, neither loving nor hating, and you may decline to offer any judgment as to my theory. But if I say, "Either accept this truth or go without it," I put on you a forced option, for there is no standing place outside of the alternative. Every dilemma based on a complete logical disjunction, with no possibility of not choosing, is an option of this forced kind. (James, 1897, p. 3)

Finally, an option may be *momentous* or *trivial*. A momentous option is one in which what you pick makes a significant difference to your life. James's example is a once-in-a-lifetime option to join a North Pole discovery expedition. You can probably think of different important choices that would have a major impact on your life.

These definitions allow James to introduce his crucial technical term: a *genuine* option is an option that is living, forced, and momentous. He then gives us his proposal, the so-called "doctrine of the will to believe":

> The thesis I defend is, briefly stated, this: *Our passional nature not only lawfully may, but must, decide an option between propositions, whenever it is a genuine option that cannot by its nature be decided on intellectual grounds; for to say, under such circumstances, "Do not decide, but leave the question open," is itself a passional decision, – just like deciding yes or no, – and is attended with the same risk of losing the truth.* (James, 1897, p. 11, original emphasis)

If an option cannot be decided on intellectual grounds, that is presumably because there is insufficient evidence in favor of either hypothesis. But if it is "lawful" or rationally permitted to believe one of these propositions, then James has described an exception to Clifford's blanket ban on belief without evidence.

What does it mean to have one's "passional nature" decide? Despite the title of the essay, James doesn't think that we can, in general, simply choose or will to believe a proposition. He asks, "Can we, by just willing it, believe that Abraham Lincoln's existence is a myth… (James, 1897, p. 4)?" James's reply is that we could *say* this but "we are absolutely impotent to believe" it. What we believe is not, in general, under our voluntary control. James is much impressed with the "magnificent edifice of the physical sciences," which he takes to have been constructed by disinterested researchers submitting to "the icy laws of outer fact" and believing what their evidence compelled them to believe (James, 1897, p. 7).

On the other hand, James writes that anyone who assumes that "pure reason is what … settles our opinions … would fly quite directly in the teeth of the facts (James, 1897, p. 8)." In fact, according to James, our "willing nature" is what determines that many options are dead for us. Moreover, many of the propositions we do accept are ones our willing natures lead us to. James elaborates,

> When I say "willing nature", I do not mean only such deliberate volitions as may have set up habits of belief that we cannot now escape from, – I mean all such factors of belief as fear and hope, prejudice and passion, imitation and partisanship, the circumpressure of our caste and set. (James, 1897, p. 9)

James first lists a few beliefs common to his caste for which he and his colleagues are unlikely to be able to give arguments: the existence of molecules, the conservation of energy, the value of democracy, the inevitability of progress, Protestant Christianity – recall that he was addressing a group of late-19th-century Ivy League philosophers – and the Monroe Doctrine. (Some of the items on this list probably could be supported; others are no doubt questionable.) He also mentions two especially interesting beliefs, namely, that *there is such a thing as truth* and that *our minds are capable of discovering it*. James holds that we cannot prove these to be true, nor can we give a convincing reply to a skeptic who denies them. Rather, we choose or will "to go in for life upon a trust or assumption which [the skeptic] does not care to make" (James, 1897, p. 10).

Thus, James thinks that we do as a matter of fact believe things we cannot prove, and his doctrine of the will to believe is supposed to show that there is nothing wrong with doing so – at least in the case of a genuine option. But why should we accept that principle? James hopes to persuade us by introducing a distinction between two intellectual duties:

Believe truths.
Avoid falsehoods.

According to James, these are not equivalent obligations. George Mavrodes (1963a) suggests that we can see the difference James has in mind by comparing two different betting strategies:

Win lots of bets.
Don't lose many bets.

Suppose you go to the race track and there are ten races on the bill. If you only bet on the sure things, or when you have a hot tip from a jockey, and decline to place bets on the rest of the races, you would emphasize the second strategy. But the more cautious you are in placing bets, the fewer bets you will win. On the other hand, if you wanted to emphasize the first strategy, you would place a bet on every race, because you can't win a bet without placing one. It's similar in the case of belief. If you emphasize James's second duty, you will only believe a proposition if it is a "sure thing." If you are cautious in this way and suspend judgment when the evidence isn't compelling, you can minimize believing falsehoods. But if you want to emphasize acquiring true beliefs, then you will be more adventurous in what you are willing to believe, adding propositions to your stock of beliefs even when the evidence doesn't compel you to do so.

James then contrasts his own position with that of Clifford's in this passage:

> Believe truth! Shun error! – these, we see, are two materially different laws; and by choosing between them we may end by coloring differently our whole intellectual life. We may regard the chase for truth as paramount, and the avoidance of error as secondary, or we may, on the other hand, treat the avoidance of error as more imperative, and let truth take its chance. Clifford … exhorts us to the latter course. Believe nothing, he tells us, keep your mind in suspense forever, rather than by closing it on insufficient evidence incur the awful risk of believing lies. You, on the other hand, may think that the risk of being in error is a very small matter when compared with the blessing of real knowledge, and be ready to be duped many times in your investigation rather than postpone indefinitely the chance of guessing true. I myself find it impossible to go with Clifford. We must remember that these feelings of our duty about either truth or error are in any case only expressions of our passional life. Biologically considered, our minds are as ready to grind out falsehood as veracity, and he who says "Better go without belief forever than believe a lie!" merely shows his own preponderant private horror of becoming a dupe. (James, 1897, p. 18)

So, why should we accept James's doctrine of the will to believe? Why should we agree that in at least the one case of a genuine option that can't be decided on the basis of evidence it is okay just to choose a hypothesis? James's answer is that this is a way of emphasizing the epistemic obligation to acquire true beliefs. If you are aiming at acquiring true beliefs and you are faced with a situation where you have to choose between propositions that have some appeal to you and where what you choose makes a significant difference to your life, then just go ahead and pick one, because that will give you a shot at getting another true belief.

An Assessment

I think it is clear that James's defense of his doctrine of the will to believe is inadequate. Even if you agree that it is better to emphasize acquiring truths rather than avoiding falsehoods, that distinction is irrelevant to the doctrine of the will to believe. In the example of the two betting strategies, there is a difference between them only if you have the option of not placing a bet. If you have to place a bet on every race, there is no way to give priority to one strategy over the other. If you bet on every race, then in every race you have a chance of winning a bet and also of losing a bet. Similarly, there is a way of emphasizing the injunction to avoid acquiring falsehoods only if "withholding" or suspending judgment – the analogue to not placing a bet – is an alternative. If you must accept one of the hypotheses, as you would have to in a forced option, there is no way to emphasize one duty at the expense of the other. If you *must* choose, you have a chance of acquiring a truth and you also have a chance of acquiring a falsehood.[3]

This merely shows that James hasn't given an adequate defense of the doctrine of the will to believe, but it doesn't show that the doctrine is mistaken. Maybe it is right. After all, how could it be wrong or irrational simply to choose to accept one of a pair of propositions in a situation in which the evidence is inconclusive but in which *you cannot avoid choosing one or the other*? If you are ever in such a situation, you certainly cannot be blamed or even chided for ending up with a belief when you couldn't help doing so. So we should consider whether the doctrine of the will to believe actually supports the rationality of theistic belief.

James had said that he was going to provide a "justification of faith." How should we apply the doctrine of the will to believe to the "religious option"? It is natural to suppose, since an option is a choice between two propositions, that the two propositions in question are:

(4)   God exists.
(5)   God does not exist.

Let us agree, for the sake of discussion, that we do not have sufficient evidence in support of either (4) or (5). This could be our tentative conclusion from the fact that we didn't find the arguments in favor of God's existence to be convincing, and we didn't find the arguments against God's existence or against the coherence of the divine attributes to be convincing, either.[4] At any rate, we weren't able to prove that (4) is true, and we weren't able to prove that (5) is true. So perhaps the option between (4) and (5) is one that can't be decided on intellectual grounds.

We may also concede, I think, that the option between (4) and (5) is momentous. For most people, whether they accept (4) or (5) makes a significant difference in their lives. And let us assume that both (4) and (5) are live (at least for those of us who are discussing these issues).

But the option between (4) and (5) is not forced. A person could avoid accepting either one of these propositions, because it is possible to suspend judgment on whether God exists.

To make this clearer, we may note that there are three possible doxastic attitudes that could be taken with respect to a proposition *p*:

Believe *p*	Believe that *p* is true
Disbelieve *p*	Believe that *p* is false
Withhold *p*	Neither believe that *p* is true nor believe that *p* is false

My office is in the Library, and I am now working in my office. So upon reflection I believe the proposition that *Someone is in the Library now*. I also disbelieve the proposition that *No one is in the Library now*. But I withhold, or suspend judgment about, the proposition that *There is an even number of people in the Library now*. I neither think that this proposition is true, nor do I think it is false (although I do think that it is one or the other).

These three options are also available when the proposition in question is the proposition that *God exists*, and they correspond to three familiar positions:

> Believe that God exists (Theism)
> Believe that God does not exist (Atheism)
> Neither believe that God exists nor believe that God does not exist (Agnosticism)

Given that there are three alternatives here, and that one can avoid taking either of the first two, it follows that the religious option is not forced and thus not a genuine option. In that case, however, James's doctrine of the will to believe, which applies only to genuine options, is useless in trying to establish the propriety of believing that God exists in the absence of compelling evidence.

In fact it is hard to see how any option, as James has defined it, could be forced. His sole example of a forced "option" – either accept this truth or go without it – is not really an option; that is, it is not a choice *between* propositions. It is a choice between *accepting* and *not accepting* a proposition. Pick nearly any *pair* of propositions that you don't already believe and it seems possible to avoid accepting either one of them.

Maybe James thinks that the religious option is forced because thinks that there is no difference between disbelieving that God exists and merely failing to believe that he does. That is, James's view seems to be that agnosticism is just the same as atheism. He writes, "We cannot escape the issue by remaining skeptical and waiting for more light, because, although we do avoid error in that way *if religion be untrue*, we lose the good, *if it be true*, just as certainly as if we positively chose to disbelieve" (James, 1897, p. 26).[5] Perhaps James's pragmatism leads him to think that positions with the same practical effects are the same. I think it is questionable that the practical effects of agnosticism really are the same as those of atheism. For one thing, an agnostic might have a reason for continued investigation into something that the atheist regards as settled. But even if James is correct in his assessment of the consequences of the two positions, he is certainly mistaken in thinking that they are therefore the same position. We can easily grasp the difference between disbelieving a proposition and declining either to believe it or disbelieve it. And thus we can agree that there is a difference between believing that (5) is true and failing to believe that (4) is false.

Perhaps there is a different way of interpreting the option according to which it really is forced. Consider the choice between these two doxastic states:

(6)   Believing that God exists
(7)   Not believing that God exists

Not believing that God exists covers the two cases of either believing that God does not exist or withholding the proposition that God exists, that is, either denying God's existence or suspending judgment about his existence. Now the choice between (6) and (7) is not a choice between propositions; rather, it is a choice between actions or states. But like James's example of "Either accept this truth or go without it," it does seem to be forced.[6] As before, let us assume that the choice between (6) and (7) is momentous and that each alternative has some appeal or is live. So in this revised interpretation, we have an option that is forced, living, and momentous. Hence, it is genuine.

Can we apply the doctrine of the will to believe to this option, and then simply will the alternative of our choice? The answer, perhaps surprisingly, is that the doctrine of the will to believe does not apply to the option between (6) and (7). We began this discussion by making the temporary assumption that there isn't sufficient evidence in favor of (4) and that there isn't sufficient evidence in favor of (5). In that case, the doxastic attitude that fits best with our evidence is to withhold both (4) and (5). Under our assumption, then, we *can* decide on intellectual grounds what to do with respect to (4) and (5). But then it follows that we can decide on intellectual grounds what to do with the forced choice between (6) and (7). Inasmuch as (7) includes withholding (4), that's the alternative our evidence supports. But the doctrine of the will to believe is explicitly restricted to genuine options that *can't* be decided on intellectual grounds. So it doesn't apply to the choice between (6) and (7).[7]

Clifford issued an evidential challenge to the rationality of theistic belief. We have seen how James tried to respond to that challenge by delineating one specific case in which it was okay to believe a proposition on insufficient evidence. But James's doctrine of the will to believe is not well defended, and it doesn't apply to the religious option, in any event. In the next chapter we'll look at a more recent attempt to reply to Clifford's challenge.

Notes

1 The story was reported by Salmon (1978). See note 20, p. 176.
2 David Hume, "Of Miracles," Section X of *An Enquiry Concerning Human Understanding*.
3 As Mavrodes notes, if there is no difference between the two intellectual duties in the case of a forced option, James is mistaken in claiming that his difference with Clifford is over which one to emphasize. Oddly, in all of the cases James mentions that aren't forced or momentous, he invariably aligns himself with Clifford and prefers to err on the side of caution. For example, James holds that "the attitude of sceptical balance is ... the absolutely wise one if we would escape mistakes. What difference, indeed, does it make to most of us whether we have or have not a theory of the Röntgen rays, whether we believe or not in mind-stuff, or have a conviction about the causality of conscious states? It makes no difference. Such options are not forced on us. On every account it is better not to make them, but still keep weighting reasons *pro et contra* with an indifferent hand" (p. 20).
4 We have not surveyed all of the arguments that have been proposed for or against God's existence, and we have not even had space to explore interesting variations on the ones we did consider. In addition, we have not raised the question of whether there could be other kinds of evidence. So I emphasize that it is at best a tentative conclusion from what we have discussed that there is not sufficient evidence for either (4) or (5).
5 James's allusions to Pascal's wager reinforce the suggestion that he thinks that the consequences of agnosticism are the same as the consequences of atheism, and thus that the practical effects of each are the same.

6   Belief, disbelief, and withholding exhaust the alternatives. (6) covers belief, and (7) covers the disjunction of disbelief and withholding. So (6) and (7) exhaust the alternatives.
7   For more on this point, see Feldman (2006), especially pp. 23–24.

Suggested Reading

Richard Feldman, "Clifford's Principle and James's Options," *Social Epistemology* 20 (1) (2006): 19–33.
George Mavrodes, "James and Clifford on 'The Will to Believe,'" *The Personalist* 44 (1963): 191–198.
Peter van Inwagen, "'It is Wrong, Everywhere, Always, and for Anyone to Believe Anything on Insufficient Evidence,'" in Jeff Jordan and Daniel Howard-Snyder, eds, *Faith, Freedom, and Rationality: Philosophy of Religion Today* (London: Rowman and Littlefield, 1996), pp. 137–153; reprinted in Eleonore Stump and Michael J. Murray, eds, *Philosophy of Religion: The Big Questions* (Oxford and Malden, MA: Blackwell, 1999), pp. 273–284.

11

The Evidentialist Objection and Foundationalism

We saw in the last chapter that Clifford's contention that "it is wrong always, everywhere, and for anyone, to believe anything upon insufficient evidence" can be adapted to yield an evidentialist objection to the rationality of theistic belief:

(1) It's rational to believe a proposition p only if there is sufficient evidence in favor of p.

(2) There isn't sufficient evidence in favor of the proposition that God exists.

∴ (3) It's not rational to believe that God exists. (1) (2)

Evidentialism and Foundationalism

In several influential papers Alvin Plantinga has taken up Clifford's challenge (Plantinga, 1981, 1983. See also Alston, 1983; Wolterstorff, 1983). He begins by exploring the notion of evidence. He notes that often we believe things *on the basis of* other beliefs. For example, my reason for believing a certain proposition might be that I believe that you testified that it was true. Or my reason for believing a proposition might be that I looked it up in what I believe to be an authoritative source. Presumably one of my beliefs is, or is part of, my justification for another belief in this way only if the former belief is itself justified. But it can't be that for every belief we have, for it to be rational or justified, it must be based on another belief that we have. There seem to be three alternatives. It could be that our belief in p is justified because we believe it on the basis of q, and our belief in q is justified because we believe it on the basis of r, and so on

The Philosophy of Religion, First Edition. Edward R. Wierenga.
© 2016 Edward R. Wierenga. Published 2016 by John Wiley & Sons, Ltd.

ad infinitum.[1] Or it could be that our belief in p is justified because we believe it on the basis of q and so on until we come to a belief, z, say, that is justified because we believe it on the basis of p. Finally, it could be that our belief in p is justified by a string of other beliefs that terminates in a belief that is not itself justified by any other belief. In the first case, our belief would depend on our believing an infinite number of other propositions, and that seems too difficult to pull off. In the second case, the justification for our belief would trace back to that very belief itself, and it's not surprising that most philosophers reject such circular reasoning. On the remaining alternative, some beliefs can be justified by other beliefs without requiring other beliefs to justify them. Some of our beliefs are *basic*, that is, believed but not on the basis of other beliefs. If we rule out infinite series and circles, it must be that some of these basic beliefs are okay to believe in this way. Such beliefs are justified or *properly basic*. It can't be, however, that just any old belief is properly basic. Some propositions, for example, *There have been more than 40 US Presidents*, demand some kind of evidential support that involves other beliefs one has, and others, say, *I am a poached egg*, are too ridiculous to be rationally believed. A challenging project is to try to specify what it takes for a proposition to be properly basic for a person.

Plantinga links this view of rational belief to "foundationalism," a traditional view in epistemology or the theory of knowledge. Historically one of the most prominent foundationalists is René Descartes (see Descartes, 1984). One naturally turns to Descartes, then, for an answer to the question of what it takes for a proposition to be properly basic. Descartes hoped to construct the "edifice" of our knowledge on a solid foundation of propositions that were so certain and secure that they were resistant to the challenge of methodological doubt. Descartes raised various possible skeptical hypotheses, for example, that one was experiencing an optical illusion, or dreaming, or being manipulated by an evil genius, according to which many of our ordinary beliefs might be false. You could believe that there is a tree in the yard but be mistaken, if an evil genius gave you the appropriate tree-like hallucination. Descartes held that although these skeptical hypotheses could cast doubt on our beliefs about the external world, they left some beliefs, for example, about our own mental states, unscathed. Perhaps the proposition that you see a tree can be doubted, but the proposition that you *seem* to see a tree (or that you are appeared to treely) escapes that skeptical doubt.[2] Plantinga characterizes such propositions as *incorrigible*, where a proposition p is incorrigible for a person S just in case (i) it is not possible that S believes p and p is false and (ii) it is not possible that S believes that p is false and yet p is true. Descartes' suggestion, then, is that propositions that are thus incorrigible are permissible to start out with; that is, they are properly basic. A second class of propositions that Descartes thought were immune from doubt, and thus certain, were propositions that are *self-evidently true*, for example, such propositions as *All triangles have three sides* or *If p is true and q is true then the conjunction of p & q is true*. For our purposes, let's say that a proposition *p* is self-evident for a person *S* just in case *S* believes *p* and it is not possible for *S* to consider *p* without seeing that *p* is true.[3] In other words, self-evident propositions are ones that if you grasp or understand them you can't help but realize that they are true. Descartes held that propositions that are self-evident for a person are also properly basic for that person.

Plantinga summarizes Descartes' view of proper basicality as follows: a proposition is properly basic for a person just in case it is either incorrigible or self-evident for that person. Plantinga claims to find a slightly different proposal in Aquinas (Plantinga, 1983, p. 57). According to Plantinga, Aquinas agreed that self-evident propositions are properly basic, but he also allowed that propositions that are "evident to the senses," such as, *There is a tree before me*, are properly basic. Combining the proposals of Descartes and Aquinas yields the principle

(4)   A proposition *p* is properly basic for a person *S* if and only if *p* is either self-evident for *S* or incorrigible for *S* or evident to the senses for *S*.

The Evidentialist Objection Restated

We began by formulating Clifford's principle as

(1)   It's rational to believe a proposition *p* only if there is sufficient evidence in favor of *p*

and then using it in an argument against the rationality of theistic belief. Our discussion (following Plantinga) of how an account of evidence might be developed suggests the following more detailed statement of Clifford's principle:

(1')   It's rational to believe a proposition *p* only if *p* is properly basic or *p* is evident with respect to propositions that are properly basic.

The idea is that some propositions are okay to start out with and that other propositions are rational to believe provided that they are supported in the right way by propositions it is rational to believe. This way of looking at things reflects Descartes' idea that our knowledge consists of an edifice erected on a foundation of certain beliefs, namely, properly basic beliefs.

If we formulate Clifford's principle as (1'), we will have to adjust the rest of the argument. Accordingly, we can add

> (5)　The proposition that God exists isn't properly basic.
> (6)　The proposition that God exists isn't evident with respect to propositions that are properly basic.

Then we can deduce, as before,

> ∴　(3)　It's not rational to believe that God exists. (1) (5) (6)

If (4) gives a correct account of what it takes to be properly basic, then it certainly seems as though premiss (5) is true. The proposition

> (7)　God exists

is not incorrigible. From Anselm's point of view, the "Fool" who "said in his heart, 'There is no God'" believes that God doesn't exist, even though he does (see Chapter 3). And atheists think that theists believe that God exists, even though he doesn't. Whether God exists or not, it's possible to have a mistaken belief about whether he does. Accordingly, (7) is not incorrigible. Moreover, (7) doesn't seem to be self-evidently true, because people are capable of grasping or considering this proposition without simply seeing that it is true. Finally, (7) is not one of those propositions that is evident to the senses or that we perceive through our senses to be true (but see Alston, 1991).

One way of conceiving of the arguments for God's existence that we considered earlier is as ways of reasoning from propositions that are properly basic to the conclusion that God exists. For example, a crucial premiss in Aquinas' cosmological argument, *Whatever begins to exist is caused to begin to exist by something already existing*, might be thought to be self-evidently true. And the premiss, *There are some contingent beings*, might be evident to the senses, or, at any rate, Aquinas' justification for that premiss, that we see things come into or go out of existence, seems to be evident to our senses. The key premiss of the ontological argument, *For all x, if x does not exist, then it is conceivable that there is something greater than x*, is plausibly thought to be self-evident. Finally, the central premiss of the argument from design,

The universe exhibits design, is the sort of claim one might think is evident to the senses. If any of these arguments were successful, then (7) would be evident with respect to propositions that are properly basic. But given that these arguments seem not to be successful, it is tempting to conclude that (7) is not evident with respect to propositions that are properly basic. So premiss (6) is true. Clifford's objection restated seems quite powerful.

Self-Referential Incoherence and Reformed Epistemology

Let's return to the argument:

> (1') It's rational to believe a proposition *p* only if *p* is properly basic or *p* is evident with respect to propositions that are properly basic.
> (5) The proposition that God exists isn't properly basic.
> (6) The proposition that God exists isn't evident with respect to propositions that are properly basic.
> ∴ (3) It's not rational to believe that God exists. (1) (5) (6)

Recall that the proposed principle explaining proper basicality, drawn from Descartes and Aquinas and which we just used in defending (5) and (6), is

> (4) A proposition *p* is properly basic for a person *S* if and only if *p* is either self-evident for *S* or incorrigible for *S* or evident to the senses for *S*.

Plantinga argues, in effect, that if (4) gives the correct account of what it takes to be properly basic, then it is not rational to believe premiss (1') of the argument (Plantinga, 1983, p. 61). It seems possible to believe that (1') is true and also possible to believe that it is false – regardless of whether it is true or false. So if (1') is true, then it is possible to believe that it is false when it is true, and if it is false it is possible to believe that it is true when it is false. Thus, (1') is not incorrigible. Moreover, (1') does not appear to be self-evidently true. Finally, (1') is not evident to the senses. Surely one could consider it and think about it without *seeing* that it is true. So if (4) is right, (1') is not properly basic. Perhaps, then, (1') could be justified or made evident by other propositions that are properly basic. But this is unpromising, as well. How could we reason from such propositions as *All bachelors are unmarried, I seem to have a headache, I see a tree in the yard*, and the like, to the conclusion that it's only rational to believe propositions that are properly basic or evident with respect to ones that are properly basic? It just is not plausible that this could be done. So if (4) is right, (1') is neither properly basic nor evident with respect to what is properly basic. In that case, if (1') is true, given what it itself says, it is not rational to believe it. (Plantinga calls this "self-referential incoherence.") It fails to satisfy its own standard. Surely it's not reasonable to be persuaded by an argument a crucial premiss of which is such that it is not rational to accept it. So if (1') is true, it's not rational to be persuaded by the argument, and, of course, if (1') is false, the argument is unsound. In either case, then, the argument fails.

What if (4) doesn't state the right conditions for a proposition's being properly basic? In that case, it's less clear that (5) and (6) are both true. If we don't know what is required for a proposition's being properly basic, how do we know that *God exists* is neither properly basic nor justified by propositions that are properly basic. The so-called Reformed epistemologists (see Plantinga, 1981, 1983; Alston, 1983; Wolterstorff, 1983)[4] hold that the proposition that God exists is in fact properly basic – a proposition that it is intellectually okay to start with, without deducing it from anything else.

We should indeed be skeptical that (4) catalogs all of the ways a proposition can be properly basic. Recall James's examples in the last chapter, *There is such a thing as [contingent] truth* and *Our minds are capable of discovering it* (James, 1897, p. 10).[5] Surely it's rational to believe these propositions, yet they don't seem to be incorrigible, self-evident, or evident to the senses, nor, as James adds, can we prove them.

There is also Bertrand Russell's famous example:

> There is no logical impossibility in the hypothesis that the world sprang into existence five minutes ago, exactly as it then was, with a population that "remembered" a wholly unreal past. There is no logically necessary connection between events at different times; therefore nothing that is happening now or will happen in the future can disprove the hypothesis that the world began five minutes ago.... I am not here suggesting that the non-existence of the past should be entertained as a serious hypothesis. Like all sceptical hypotheses, it is logically tenable but uninteresting. (Russell, 1921, pp. 159–160)

It is certainly rational, as Russell thinks, to believe that the world has existed for more than five minutes. But if all we have to go on are propositions that are incorrigible (typically about our own current mental states), propositions that are self-evident (because they involve necessary connections between ideas), and propositions reporting our present perceptions, it is hard to see how we could justify our belief in the past. As Russell noted, "everything constituting a memory-belief is happening now, not in that past time to which the belief is said to refer." There is nothing about our current state that guarantees that those musty books in the library have been there for years rather than having been created, along with the rest of the world and its apparent traces of a distant past, a mere five minutes ago.

A final example: we often believe things because we remember them. I believe that I picked up the mail this morning because I remember picking it up. I don't focus on the memory and then reason to the conclusion that since I have the memory it's likely that the proposition is true. Rather, in the presence of the memory experience I simply believe that I picked up the mail. But the proposition that I picked up the mail this morning is not incorrigible, self-evident to me, or evident to my senses. So (4) is too limiting in what should count as properly basic. Is there a sensible way of expanding it that would permit belief in God to be properly basic? Before we try to answer that question, let's consider a more recent development in religious epistemology.

Warrant and Proper Function

Alvin Plantinga and other Reformed epistemologists claim that belief in God might be properly basic. For all we have seen so far, however, this is really just a conjecture, one that emerges once it is recognized that historically prominent standards for what is properly basic are too restrictive. Some additional beliefs have to be recognized as properly basic, in any event, so maybe the belief that God exists should be admitted to the club. More recently, however, Plantinga has offered positive support for the claim that belief in God is properly basic by developing a detailed theory of knowledge that has this as a consequence (at least if God exists).

To better appreciate Plantinga's theory, we should first contrast it with a more traditional view. In the *Theaetetus* (369 BCE) Plato inaugurated a long philosophical tradition by asking what knowledge is. One of the ways Plato addressed this question was by asking what must be added to mere true opinion to get knowledge. The person who merely has a *true belief* about which is the right road to the destination is just as likely to get there as the person who *knows* which is the right road; so, what is distinctive of knowledge? An answer Plato considered, but left unsettled, is that knowledge is true belief plus an account of what makes the belief true. Subsequent philosophers, especially those in the late 20th century developed Plato's suggestion and held that knowledge is justified true belief (together with an additional factor to avoid certain objections).[6] The idea, then, is that knowledge requires justification, and the standard way of thinking of justification is that it requires having the right kind of evidence.

Plantinga does not think that justification is either necessary or (together with true belief) sufficient for knowledge. Rather, he adapts Plato's formula but introduces a new concept, *warrant*, which he says is "that further quality or quantity ... enough of which distinguishes knowledge from mere true belief" (Plantinga, 2000, p. 153). The unique feature of Plantinga's approach is his insistence that warranted beliefs *arise* in a certain way, namely, by one's cognitive, belief-forming faculties *functioning properly*. Plantinga's summary:

> Put in a nutshell, then, a belief has warrant for a person S only if that belief is produced in S by cognitive faculties functioning properly (subject to no dysfunction) in a cognitive environment that is appropriate for S's kind of cognitive faculties, according to a design plan that is successfully aimed at truth. (Plantinga, 2000, p. 156)

A belief thus has warrant for a person just in case that belief is produced by a cognitive process, for example, perception or memory or a faculty that responds to testimony, that is functioning properly, according to a design that is successfully aimed at producing true beliefs.[7] In addition, the process in question must be operating in the sort of circumstances for which it was designed to operate; in the case of perception, for example, the circumstances include adequate lighting on medium-sized objects in the near vicinity and no recent ingestion of hallucinogens. According to Plantinga, then, when a true belief has sufficient warrant (in this sense), it counts as knowledge.

According to this theory, perception is a cognitive process, and when it is functioning properly it produces in us beliefs about what we perceive. If you perceive a tree, you don't have to reason from the allegedly incorrigible proposition, *I seem to see a tree*, to the proposition about the external world, *There is a tree*. Rather, belief in the latter proposition arises automatically if our perceptual faculty is functioning properly when we look at a tree. If we are in the sort of circumstances for which our perceptual faculty was designed to operate, then we are warranted in our belief that there is a tree. This theory also gives an answer to the question we raised above about memory. Memory is another cognitive process, successfully aimed at truth; so if I remember picking up the mail, then I am warranted in my belief that I picked up the mail. And if I remember things from many years ago, then I am warranted in believing that they happened many years ago, from which I can deduce that the world has existed for more than five minutes.

Plantinga also thinks that (if God exists) we have been designed to find ourselves with the belief that God exists. Following John Calvin, he holds that we have another cognitive faculty, a *sensus divinitatis* or sense of divinity, which, when functioning properly, produces in us the belief that God exists. If this cognitive faculty is successfully aimed at truth and operating in the circumstances for which it was designed to operate, then a person who acquires the belief that God exists in this way is warranted in that belief, and, on the assumption that it is true that God exists, such a person can *know* that God exists.[8]

According to Plantinga's view, a basic belief formed by properly functioning cognitive faculties (operating according to a design plan successfully aimed at truth in circumstances in which they were designed to operate) is *automatically* properly basic. His account of warrant as proper functioning thus fills in the details of how belief in God can be properly basic. The person who acquires the belief that God exists through a properly functioning epistemic faculty, the *sensus divinitatis*, believes that God exists without basing this belief on other beliefs, and given that the belief is warranted, it is properly basic. Accordingly, this theory gives Plantinga a reason to deny

(5)   The proposition that God exists isn't properly basic.

That is, it gives him a reason to deny this premiss of the evidentialist objection.

Warrant and Defeat

Some philosophers have argued that even if belief in God is properly basic, it can still be *defeated*. A defeater for a proposition one is justified (or warranted) in believing is new evidence or information that makes one no longer justified (or warranted). John Pollack distinguished a *rebutting* defeater from an *undercutting* defeater (Pollock, 1974). The former is new evidence that counts against a proposition one believes, that is, new evidence against the *truth* of the proposition. The latter is new evidence that undermines one's justification or evidence for a proposition one believes. For example, evidence that a red light is shining on an object that appears red to you undermines your justification for thinking that the object is red, but it is not evidence that the object isn't red. So in this case we have an undercutting defeater but not a rebutting defeater.

According to Plantinga's account of warrant as proper functioning, as we have seen, any proposition you come to believe in the basic way through properly functioning cognitive faculties is properly basic. But such beliefs can be defeated; they are not immune to revision. If I think I remember bringing in the mail, then, in typical circumstances, the proposition that I brought in the mail is warranted for me and properly basic. But if I then discover that there is no mail on the desk but that there are letters and magazines in the mailbox, my new evidence defeats my earlier belief that I brought in the mail.

Plantinga examines a variety of potential defeaters for theistic belief (Plantinga, 2000, pp. 367–499; 2015, chapters 8–10). He concludes that they do not succeed. His discussion of these putative defeaters is interesting and insightful, but his case against them receives an extra boost because he is able to appeal to his own, distinctive account of defeat. For Plantinga, defeat, like warrant itself, is to be understood in terms of properly functioning cognitive faculties. According to his view, roughly stated, a proposition *d* is a defeater for someone's belief *b* just in case anyone who believes *b* and whose cognitive faculties are functioning properly gives up the belief that *b* upon acquiring a belief in the new proposition *d*.[9] Suppose you seem to see a sheep in the field and so you come to believe that there is a sheep in the field. Then the owner of the field, whom you know to be trustworthy, tells you that there are never any sheep in that field but that the neighbor's sheepdog looks like a sheep and likes to hang out there. You then come to believe that there are no sheep in the field, and, given that your cognitive faculties are functioning properly, they jettison your earlier belief that there is a sheep in the field.

According to Plantinga, typical theists come to have their theistic belief through the proper functioning of their cognitive faculties and are thus warranted in them, and if typical theists reasonably come to believe a putative defeater for their belief that God exists, for example, that the world contains a lot of apparently pointless suffering, they nevertheless remain warranted in their theistic belief. Their cognitive faculties properly retain the belief the belief that God exists. As Plantinga puts it, "the very fact that [the person] continues in theistic belief is evidence that the *sensus divinitatis* is functioning properly to at least some degree in her, and in such a way that knowledge of the facts of evil does not constitute a defeater" (Plantinga, 2000, p. 491).

I myself am not persuaded that it is the proper functioning of one's cognitive faculties that determines whether one has knowledge of a proposition or is justified in believing a proposition, as I'll try to explain in the next section. I think one's evidence plays a more crucial role in knowledge.

In addition, I don't think that defeat is best understood in terms of proper functioning – unless what proper functioning epistemic faculties do is assess the evidential force of putative defeaters. So I can't simply endorse Plantinga's rejection of defeaters for theistic belief. I'll try to say later what I think instead. But, first, in the next section I'll raise an objection to the proper functioning account of warrant.

Warrant, What's It Good For?[10]

Why should we think that acquiring a belief through one's cognitive faculties functioning properly according to a design plan successfully aimed at truth is what it takes for a belief to be rational or, if it is true, to count as knowledge? What if that design plan has our cognitive faculties deliver true beliefs all right, but they do so in the absence of appropriate evidence? Here's a simple example. We regularly form beliefs about what time it is by looking at clocks or by hearing bells strike the hour. We don't engage in a process of reasoning; for example, we don't think, "The big hand is pointing to the 12 and the little hand is pointing to the 3, therefore, it is 3 o'clock." Rather, we look at the clock and simply believe that it is 3 o'clock. Now every spring we turn our clocks forward an hour to observe daylight savings time. Suppose that God had designed us differently so that we didn't have to change our clocks but that our cognitive faculties change instead, producing beliefs differently, depending on the season. In the winter when we see a clock we reasonably take to be accurate that indicates 3 o'clock, we automatically form the belief that it is now 3 o'clock. In the summer, when we see the same clock in the same configuration, we automatically form the belief that it is now 4 o'clock. During the summer we could thus have a true belief about the current time produced by our cognitive faculties functioning properly according to a design plan successfully aimed at truth, but I don't think that we would *know* that it is 4 o'clock if we got our belief in this way.[11] If we were asked to justify our belief that it is 4 o'clock now, we could only point to a clock that displayed a different time.

Perhaps this example would lose some plausibility if we had to flesh it out more fully. What would we believe in the summer about the positions of the hands on the face of the clock, or what would we say about how many times the bells rang? Would we get these things right? So let's try another example, one that involves a global disconnect from the evidence. Suppose, to keep things simpler, that we live on an island. Somewhere, far away and inaccessible to us, is another island, a virtual duplicate of the one we inhabit, including trees and houses corresponding to our trees and houses and avatars corresponding to each of us. Suppose that God's design plan for us is that whenever we perceive something on our island we automatically get a true belief about the inaccessible island. God is careful to make sure that what happens on the inaccessible island exactly parallels what happens on our island. So we acquire lots of true beliefs in the usual ways, including through perception, memory, testimony, etc., except that most of our beliefs are about what is going on or what things are like on the inaccessible island.[12] In this way, then, we acquire true beliefs through our cognitive faculties functioning properly in the way God designed them to operate. But I don't think that we *know* things about what is happening on the inaccessible island. We don't know, for example, that there is a tree in the front yard of the house (on the inaccessible island) when our perception is of a tree and house on our own island. Thus, having been formed by cognitive faculties functioning properly according to a design plan successfully aimed at truth does not suffice to turn a true belief into knowledge. The proper functioning account of warrant seems to me to be misguided.[13]

An Evidentialist Alternative

I wish I could offer a compelling alternative account that shows that theistic belief is rational, but I don't have a developed rival view. I think, however, that a partial answer is to be found by noticing that we often find ourselves believing certain things, and the fact that we have such beliefs is itself evidence that they are true. I find myself with the belief that I brought the mail in, and that is a reason to think that I did. Richard Swinburne calls this "the principle of credulity."

Theists typically find themselves with the belief that God exists. It's rare, but not unheard of, for someone to believe in God's existence on the basis of the kinds of arguments we considered earlier. But for someone who believes that God exists without basing that belief on argument or on other beliefs for which the person has evidence, perhaps simply having the belief is some reason to think that it is true. Of course, this can't be the whole story. There could be some reason to think that a belief is true but other reasons to think that it is false. Swinburne recognizes this possibility when he adds an important qualification: "the mere fact that one has a basic belief is a reason for believing it to be true and so in the absence of contrary evidence it is a justified basic belief" (Swinburne, 2010, p. 682). A belief one finds oneself with can be justified, provided that there isn't sufficiently compelling counter-evidence.

Most contemporary theists recognize that not everyone shares their belief and they are, moreover, familiar with objections to theistic belief. Such believers, thus, find themselves with the belief that God exists but they are aware of putative defeaters, or potential contrary evidence, for that belief. If Swinburne's second condition, that there not be sufficiently compelling contrary evidence, isn't satisfied, then the belief that God exists won't be properly basic.[14] But if the putative defeaters can themselves be defeated, or if the potential contrary evidence turns out not to be sufficiently compelling, then the belief that God exists can be properly basic. In that case, there is, in addition, a reason to deny premiss (5) of the evidentialist objection.[15]

This way of thinking about matters provides a perspective for what we have been able to accomplish in this book. We didn't find the leading arguments in favor of God's existence to be successful. But the widespread existence of evil and suffering, the alleged incoherence of omnipotence, the alleged incompatibility of foreknowledge and free will or of divine freedom and perfect goodness, and the evidentialist challenge to theistic belief are all putative defeaters of belief in God. What I hope we have seen is that these putative defeaters are not successful defeaters – they do not succeed in undermining the rationality of belief in God.

Perhaps this is the most one can reasonably expect of philosophy of religion. Aquinas, for example, held that sacred doctrine

> disputes argumentatively with one who denies its principles only if the opponent admits some at least of the truths obtained through divine revelation. Thus, we can argue with heretics from texts in Holy Scripture, and against those who deny one article of faith we can argue from another. If our opponent believes nothing of divine revelation, there is no longer any means of proving the articles of faith by argument, but only of answering his objections – if he has any – against faith. Since faith rests upon infallible truth, and since the contrary of a truth can never be demonstrated, it is clear that the proofs brought against faith are not demonstrations, but arguments that can be answered. (Aquinas, 1948 [1485], *Summa Theologiae*, I, 1, 8)

If it is true that God exists, then there are no good proofs of his non-existence. Whether there are or are not such proofs is something best discovered by looking carefully at the kinds of objections that have been raised against theism, which is what we have attempted to do. If we have been successful, we have shown that these objections "can be answered."

One final thought: philosophy of religion considers questions that are fun to think about, and it often employs philosophical tools and techniques that are interesting in their own right. One therefore does not have to be a theist to be interested in philosophy of religion. But for the religious believer philosophy of religion can play an additional role, one described by William Alston:

> Philosophical thinking can enable us to see through objections to Christian belief; it can exhibit the faith as something plausible and intellectually respectable; it can show the faith as something that can command the assent of an educated, intellectually sophisticated, and knowledgeable denizen of the late twentieth century.... [P]hilosophical thinking can play a crucial role in coming to a deeper understanding of the faith. "Faith seeking understanding" is [an important] motto.... But when faith is seeking understanding, the faith is already there, and philosophy comes on the scene too late to produce it. (Alston, 1994, pp. 26–27)

Notes

1   Where each of *p*, *q*, etc., is distinct from the others.
2   The locution "appeared to F-ly" is due to Roderick Chisholm. See, for example, his *Theory of Knowledge*, 2nd edn (Chisholm, 1977), p. 30.
3   Compare Aquinas's remarks on self-evidence:

> A thing can be self-evident in either of two ways: on the one hand, self-evident in itself, though not to us; on the other, self-evident in itself, and to us. A proposition is self-evident because the predicate is included in the essence of the subject: e.g., *Man is an animal*, for animal is contained in the essence of man. If, therefore, the essence of the predicate and the subject be known to all, the proposition will be self-evident to all, as is clear with regard to the first principles of demonstration, the terms of which are certain common notions that no one is ignorant of, such as being and non-being, whole and part, and the like. If, however there are some to whom the essence of the predicate and subject is unknown, the proposition will be self-evident in itself, but not to those who do not know the meaning of the predicate and subject of the proposition. Therefore, it happens, as Boethius says, that there are some notions of the mind which are common and self-evident only to the learned, as that incorporeal substances are not in space. (Aquinas, 1948 [1485], *Summa Theologiae*, I, 2, 1)

The person "to whom the essence of the predicate and subject is unknown" is someone who, according to the definition given in the text, doesn't grasp or understand the proposition expressed in those terms and thus doesn't *see* that the proposition is true.

4   The term "Reformed epistemologist" comes from the fact some of these phi-
    losophers found sources for this view in the work of some Reformed theolo-
    gians, that is, theologians standing in the tradition of John Calvin, and from
    the fact that several of them were associated with Calvin College, an institu-
    tion in that same tradition.

5   I've inserted the restriction to *contingent* truth (which I think James intend-
    ed) because some necessary truths, for example, propositions of elementary
    arithmetic or basic logic, are self-evident to us; and it might also be the case
    that it is self-evident to us that they are self-evident to us, from which we can
    deduce that our minds are capable of discovering them.

6   For a survey of attempts to analyze knowledge in this tradition, see Shope
    (1983).

7   Plantinga thinks that our cognitive faculties have been designed by God, a feature
    to which I will appeal in framing an objection in the section titled "Warrant:
    What's It Good For?." But he holds that one could understand cognitive faculties
    being designed for something without acknowledging a divine designer.

8   In *Knowledge and Christian Belief* (Plantinga, 2015) Plantinga qualifies this,
    saying that it is only in the *ideal* case, where the belief has a lot of warrant,
    that the believer *knows* that God exists. In typical cases of theistic belief, the
    believer has enough warrant to be rational in holding the belief, even it if falls
    short of knowledge.

9   I am oversimplifying Plantinga's account of defeat. For an elaborate attempt
    at definition, see Plantinga (2000), p. 363.

10 My objection is not to Plato's idea of that which when added to true belief
    yields knowledge; rather, it is to the claim that the appeal to properly func-
    tioning cognitive faculties explains it.

11 I am assuming that our beliefs about what time it is arise automatically when
    we look at a clock. The case would be different if we reasoned to a conclusion
    about the time. For example, we sometimes forget to change a clock and thus
    think, "The clock says 3 o'clock but it wasn't properly set forward; so when
    it says 3:00 it is really 4:00. Therefore it is now 4 o'clock."

12 It is only our beliefs about what transpires in the vicinity of the inaccessible
    island that I claim do not constitute knowledge. Our beliefs about the sun,
    moon, and stars, for example, could be about those actual things, and, if we
    are justified in believing them and they are true, would be known to us. If
    you don't think that the propositions we believe in this story properly hook
    up with our avatars and the other things on the inaccessible island, add to the
    story that we start life on the inaccessible island, occupying a position inside
    the heads of our avatars through which we acquire a first-person perspective
    about our surroundings and acquire concepts that apply to the things there.
    We are then transported unknowingly to our own island, with our beliefs
    continuing to be about things on the now inaccessible island.

13 Here's another example, perhaps slightly less far-fetched, due to John Bennett.
    Suppose that God has created some other rational creatures on a planet that

orbits a star that is visible from earth. Because God wants human beings to discover these other creatures, he designs the cognitive faculties of some human beings to produce the true belief, *There are rational creatures in the vicinity of that star*, whenever one of these human beings looks at that star. The belief is true and produced by cognitive faculties functioning properly in the way they were designed to function, but this belief isn't knowledge.

14   This second condition is what rules out the simple-minded objection to this view that if belief in God is properly basic, then any wacky belief would also have to be judged to be properly basic. A literature has developed defending the "Great Pumpkin" objection or variations on Bertrand Russell's teapot in space. The Peanuts comic strip character Linus believes that the quasi-religious Great Pumpkin will appear on Halloween. Russell imagined a very small, undetectable china teapot in orbit around the sun between the earth and Mars (Russell, 1952, pp. 543–548). If someone believed in the Great Pumpkin or in Russell's teapot, without basing that belief on evidence, would that belief be properly basic? Presumably not, because we have an impressive amount of evidence about the origins of pumpkins and their lack of agency and mobility, and we have a similar amount of evidence about the manufacture or production of teapots and of which rockets have launched which artifacts into orbit, evidence that defeats, respectively, belief in the Great Pumpkin or in Russell's teapot.

15   Todd Long has suggested to me that Paul Moser's work can be read as proposing a different account of how the belief that God exists can be properly basic. See Moser (2010). Moser suggests that one might experience "God's intervening Spirit at work in one's motivational center, leading one away from selfishness and toward unselfish love" (p. 199). Perhaps, then, one finds oneself not simply with the belief that God exists but with the experience of God at work in one's heart. On the other hand, Moser seems to take this experience as evidence. He writes, "The best explanation of our new lives ... will be that God has indeed visited us redemptively, and that is evidence enough" (p. 230). According to this construal, we *reason to the conclusion* that God exists as the best explanation of our felt moral reorientation.

Suggested Reading

Alvin Plantinga, "Reason and Belief in God," in Alvin Plantinga and Nicholas Wolterstorff, eds, *Faith and Rationality: Reason and Belief in God* (Notre Dame, IN: University of Notre Dame Press, 1983), pp. 16–93.

Alvin Plantinga, *Knowledge and Christian Belief* (Grand Rapids, MI: William B. Eerdmans, 2015).

Linda Zagzebski, "Religious Knowledge and the Virtues of the Mind," in Linda Zagzebski, ed., *Rational Faith: Catholic Responses to Reformed Epistemology* (Notre Dame, IN: University of Notre Dame Press, 1993), pp. 199–225.

References

Robert M. Adams, "Must God Create the Best?" *Philosophical Review* 81 (1972): 317–332; reprinted in his *The Virtue of Faith and Other Essays in Philosophical Theology* (New York: Oxford University Press, 1987), pp. 51–64.

William P. Alston, "Christian Experience and Christian Belief," in Alvin Plantinga and Nicholas Wolterstorff, eds, *Faith and Rationality: Reason and Belief in God* (Notre Dame, IN: University of Notre Dame Press, 1983), pp. 103–134.

William P. Alston, "Does God Have Beliefs?" *Religious Studies* 22 (1987): 287–306; reprinted in his *Divine Nature and Human Language: Essays in Philosophical Theology* (Ithaca, NY: Cornell University Press, 1989).

William P. Alston, *Perceiving God* (Ithaca, NY: Cornell University Press, 1991).

William P. Alston, "A Philosopher's Way Back," in Thomas V. Morris, ed., *God and the Philosophers: The Reconciliation of Faith and Reason* (Oxford: Oxford University Press, 1994), pp. 19–30.

Anselm of Canterbury, *The Major Works*, Brian Davies and G. G. Evans, eds (Oxford and New York: Oxford University Press, 1998).

Thomas Aquinas, *Summa Theologiae*, in Anton Pegis, ed., *Introduction to St. Thomas Aquinas* (New York: Modern Library, 1948).

Thomas Aquinas, *Summa Contra Gentiles*, I, 2, 25, A. C. Pegis, trans. (Notre Dame, IN: University of Notre Dame Press, 1975).

Augustine, *City of God*, Marcus Dods, trans. (New York: Modern Library, 1950).

Augustine, *On Free Choice of the Will*, Thomas Williams, trans. (Indianapolis, IN: Hackett Publishing, 1993).

Avicenna, *The Physics of the Healing*, Bk III, chapter 11, Jon McGinnis, trans. (Provo, UT: Brigham Young University Press, 2009).

Lynne R. Baker and Gareth B. Matthews, "Anselm's Argument Reconsidered," *The Review of Metaphysics* 64(1) (2010): 31–54.

Max Baker-Hytch, "Religious Diversity and Epistemic Luck," *International Journal for Philosophy of Religion* 76 (2014): 171–191.

The Philosophy of Religion, First Edition. Edward R. Wierenga.
© 2016 Edward R. Wierenga. Published 2016 by John Wiley & Sons, Ltd.

David Blumenfeld, "On the Compossibility of the Divine Attributes," *Philosophical Studies* 34(1) (1978): 91–103.

Anicius Manlius Severinus Boethius, *The Consolation of Philosophy*, Richard Green, trans. (Indianapolis, IN: Bobbs-Merrill, 1962).

Pascal Boyer, *Religion Explained: The Evolutionary Foundations of Religious Belief* (New York: Basic Books, 2001).

Rudolph Bultmann, "New Testament and Mythology," in H. W. Bartsch, ed. and R. H. Fuller, trans., *Kerygma and Myth: A Theological Debate* (New York: Harper & Row, 1961).

John Jefferson Davis, "The Design Argument, Cosmic 'Fine-tuning,' and the Anthropic Principle," *International Journal of Philosophy of Religion* 22 (1987): 139–150.

Roderick Chisholm, *Theory of Knowledge*, 2nd edn (Englewood Cliffs, NJ: Prentice-Hall, 1977).

Alonzo Church, *Introduction to Mathematical Logic* (Princeton, NJ: Princeton University Press, 1956).

Samuel Clarke, *Discourse Concerning the Unchangeable Obligations of Natural Religion and the Truth and Certainty of the Christian Religion*, 4th edn (London: Printed by Will Botham, for James Knapton, at the Crown in St. Paul's churchyard, 1716).

William Kingdon Clifford, "Ethics of Belief," in Leslie Stephen and Frederick Pollack, eds, *Lectures and Essays*, Vol. II (London: Macmillan, 1979), pp. 177–211.

Robin Collins, "A Scientific Argument for the Existence of God," in Michael Murray, ed., *Reason for the Hope Within* (Grand Rapids, MI: Wm. B. Eerdmans, 1999), pp. 47–75.

Earl Conee, "The Possibility of Power beyond Possibility," in James Tomberlin, ed., *Philosophical Perspectives, 5, Philosophy of Religion* (Atascadero, CA: Ridgeview Press, 1991): pp. 447–473.

René Descartes, *Meditations on First Philosophy* in John Cottingham, Robert Stoothoff, and Dugald Murdoch, trans., *The Philosophical Writings of Descartes*, Vol. 2 (Cambridge: Cambridge University Press, 1984).

Trent Dougherty, *The Problem of Animal Pain: A Theodicy for All Creatures Great and Small* (London: Palgrave Macmillan, 2014).

Trent Dougherty and Justin P. McBrayer, eds, *Skeptical Theism: New Essays* (Oxford: Oxford University Press, 2014).

Paul Draper, "Pain and Pleasure: An Evidential Problem for Theists," *Noûs* 23 (1989): 331–350.

Émile Durkheim, *The Elementary Forms of the Religious Life* [1912], Joseph Ward Swain, trans. (London: Allen and Unwin, 1976).

Richard Feldman, "Clifford's Principle and James's Options," *Social Epistemology* 20(1) (2006): 19–33.

John Martin Fisher, ed., *God, Foreknowledge, and Freedom* (Stanford, CA: Stanford University Press, 1989).

Thomas Flint, "The Problem of Divine Freedom," *American Philosophical Quarterly* 20 (1983): 255–264.

Thomas Flint, *Divine Providence: The Molinist Account* (Ithaca, NY: Cornell University Press, 1998).

Harry Frankfurt, "The Logic of Omnipotence," *The Philosophical Review* 73 (1964): 262–263.

Sigmund Freud, *The Future of an Illusion* [1927], W. D. Robson-Scott, trans. (Garden City, NY: Doubleday, 1964).

Peter Geach, *Providence and Evil* (Cambridge: Cambridge University Press, 1977).

Lenn E. Goodman, *Avicenna* (London and New York: Routledge, 1992), p. 186.

Robert Hambourger, "Belief in Miracles and Hume's Essay," *Noûs* 14 (1980): 587–604.

Charles Hartshorne, *Anselm's Discovery* (LaSalle, IL: Open Court, 1967).

William Hasker, *Providence, Evil and the Openness of God* (London and New York: Routledge, 2004).

Ernest Hemingway, *A Moveable Feast* (New York: Charles Scribner's Sons, 1964).

R. F. Holland, "The Miraculous," *American Philosophical Quarterly* 2 (1965): 43–51.

Daniel Howard-Snyder, *The Evidential Argument from Evil* (Bloomington and Indianapolis, IN: Indiana University Press, 1996).

Daniel Howard-Snyder, "The Puzzle of Prayers of Thanksgiving and Praise," in Yujin Nagasawa and Erik J. Wielenberg, eds, *New Waves in Philosophy of Religion* (New York: Palgrave Macmillan, 2009), pp. 125–149.

David Hume, *Dialogues Concerning Natural Religion*, Norman Kemp Smith, ed. (Indianapolis, IN: Bobbs-Merrill, 1947).

David Hume, *An Enquiry Concerning Human Understanding*, in L. A. Selby-Bigge, ed., *Enquiries Concerning Human Understanding and Concerning the Principles of Morals*, 3rd edn, revised by P. H. Nidditch (Oxford: Clarendon Press, 1975).

David Hume, "Of Miracles," Section X, *An Enquiry Concerning Human Understanding* (1777), in L. A. Selby-Bigge, ed., *Enquiries Concerning Human Understanding and Concerning the Principles of Morals*, 3rd edn, revised by P. H. Nidditch (Oxford: Clarendon Press, 1975).

William James, "The Will to Believe," in his *The Will to Believe, and Other Essays in Popular Philosophy* (New York: Longmans, Green and Co., 1897).

Immanuel Kant, *Critique of Pure Reason*, Norman Kemp Smith, trans. (London: Macmillan, 1929).

Garrison Keillor, "Zeus the Lutheran," *The New Yorker*, October 29 (1990): 32–37.

Anthony Kenny, *The Five Ways: Aquinas' Proofs of God's Existence* (London: Routledge and Kegan Paul, 1969; reprinted South Bend, IN: University of Notre Dame Press, 1980).

Klaas Kraay, "Can God Satisfice?," *American Philosophical Quarterly* 50(4) (2013): 399–410.

Norman Kretzmann, "Omniscience and Immutability," *Journal of Philosophy* 63(14) (1966): 409–421.

Norman Kretzmann, "A Particular Problem of Creation," in Scott MacDonald, ed., *Being and Goodness* (Ithaca, NY: Cornell University Press, 1991), pp. 229–249.

Saul Kripke, *Reference and Existence* (Oxford: Oxford University Press, 2013).

Brian Leftow, "Omnipotence," in Thomas P. Flint and Michael C. Rea, eds, *The Oxford Handbook of Philosophical Theology* (Oxford: Oxford University Press, 2009), pp. 167–193.

Gottfried Wilhelm Leibniz, *Theodicy: Essays on the Goodness of God, the Freedom on Man and the Origin of Evil*, E. M. Huggard, trans. (La Salle, IL: Open Court, 1985).

Gottfried Wilhelm Leibniz, "Fourth Letter to Samuel Clark," in G. W. Leibniz and Samuel Clark, *Correspondence*, Roger Ariew, ed. (Indianapolis, IN: Hackett Publishing Company, 2000).

C. S. Lewis, *Mere Christianity* (New York: Macmillan, 1953).

C. S. Lewis, *The Problem of Pain* (New York: Macmillan, 1962).

David Lewis, *On the Plurality of Worlds* (Oxford: Basil Blackwell, 1986).

Titus Livy, *The History of Rome, Books 1–5 (Ab Urbe Condita, Liber 1–5)*, Valerie M. Warrior, trans. (Indianapolis, IN: Hackett Publishing Company, 2006).

Moses Maimonides, *Guide for the Perplexed*, M. Friedlander, trans. (London: George Routledge & Sons, 1904).

Norman Malcolm, "Anselm's Ontological Arguments," *Philosophical Review* 69 (1960): 41–62.

J. L. Mackie, "Evil and Omnipotence," *Mind* 64 (1955): 200–212.

J. L. Mackie, *The Miracle of Theism* (Oxford: The Clarendon Press, 1982).

George Mavrodes, "James and Clifford on 'The Will to Believe'," *The Personalist* 44 (1963a): 191–198.

George Mavrodes, "Some Puzzles concerning Omnipotence," *The Philosophical Review* 72 (1963b): 221–223.

George Mavrodes, *Belief in God* (New York: Random House, 1970).

Luis de Molina, *Of Divine Foreknowledge (Part IV of the Concordia)*, Alfred Freddoso, intro. and trans. (Ithaca, NY: Cornell University Press, 1988).

Paul Moser, *The Evidence for God: Religious Knowledge Reexamined* (Cambridge: Cambridge University Press, 2010).

Michael J. Murray, *Nature Red in Tooth and Claw: Theism and the Problem of Animal Suffering* (Oxford: Oxford University Press, 2008).

William of Ockham, *Predestination, God's Foreknowledge, and Future Contingents*, 2nd edn, Marilyn McCord Adams and Norman Kretzmann, trans. (Indianapolis, IN: Hackett, 1983).

William Paley, *Natural Theology; or, Evidences of the Existence and Attributes of the Deity* (Philadelphia, PA: Printed for John Morgan by H. Maxwell, 1802).

Michael Peterson, William Hasker, Bruce Reichenbach, and David Basinger, eds, *Philosophy of Religion Selected Readings*, 5th edition (Oxford: Oxford University Press, 2014).

Nelson Pike, "Divine Omniscience and Voluntary Action," *Philosophical Review* 74 (1965): 27–46.

Nelson Pike, "Of God and Freedom: A Rejoinder," *Philosophical Review* 75 (1966): 369–379.

Nelson Pike, "Omnipotence and God's Ability to Sin," *American Philosophical Quarterly* 6(3) (1969): 208–216.

Clark Pinnock, Richard Rice, John Sanders, William Hasker, and David Basinger, *The Openness of God: A Biblical Challenge to the Traditional Understanding of God* (Downers Grove, IL: InterVarsity Press, 1994).

Alvin Plantinga, *The Nature of Necessity* (Oxford: Clarendon Press, 1974).

Alvin Plantinga, *God, Freedom, and Evil* (New York: Harper and Row, 1974; reprinted Grand Rapids, MI: Wm. B. Eerdmans, 1977).

Alvin Plantinga, "Is Belief in God Properly Basic?," *Noûs* 15 (1981): 41–53.

Alvin Plantinga, "Reason and Belief in God," in Alvin Plantinga and Nicholas Wolterstorff, eds, *Faith and Rationality: Reason and Belief in God* (Notre Dame, IN: University of Notre Dame Press, 1983), pp. 16–93.

Alvin Plantinga, "On Ockham's Way Out," *Faith and Philosophy* 3 (1986): 235–269

Alvin Plantinga, *Warranted Christian Belief* (Oxford: Oxford University Press, 2000).

Alvin Plantinga, *Knowledge and Christian Belief* (Grand Rapids, MI: Wm B. Eerdmans, 2015).

John Pollock, *Knowledge and Justification* (Princeton, NJ: Princeton University Press, 1974).

Michael Rea and Louis Pojman, eds, *Philosophy of Religion: An Anthology*, 7th edn (Stamford, CT: Cengage Learning, 2015).

W. D. Ross, *The Right and the Good* (Oxford: Oxford University Press, 2002).

William Rowe, "The Problem of Evil and Some Varieties of Atheism," *American Philosophical Quarterly* 16 (1979): 335–341.

William Rowe, "The Problem of Divine Perfection and Freedom," in Eleonore Stump, ed., *Reasoned Faith* (Ithaca, NY: Cornell University Press, 1993), pp. 223–233.

William Rowe, "The Evidential Argument from Evil: A Second Look," in Daniel Howard-Snyder, ed., *The Evidential Argument from Evil* (Bloomington and Indianapolis, IN: Indiana University Press, 1996), pp. 262–285.

William Rowe, "Can God Be Free?," *Faith and Philosophy* 19(4) (2002): 405–424.

William Rowe, *Can God Be Free?* (Oxford: Oxford University Press, 2004).

Richard Rubenstein, *After Auschwitz: Radical Theology and Contemporary Judaism* (Indianapolis, IN: Bobbs-Merrill, 1966).

Bertrand Russell, *The Analysis of Mind* (London: George Allen and Unwin, 1921).

Bertrand Russell, "Is There a God?" (1952), in John G. Slater and Peter Köllner, eds, *The Collected Papers of Bertrand Russell, Volume 11: Last Philosophical Testament, 1943–68* (London: Routledge, 1997), pp. 543–548.

Bruce Russell, "Defenseless," in Daniel Howard-Snyder, ed., *The Evidential Argument from Evil* (Bloomington and Indianapolis, IN: Indiana University Press, 1996), pp. 193–205.

Saadia Gaon, *The Book of Beliefs and Opinions, Treatise VII* (variant), Samuel Rosenblatt, trans. (New Haven, CT: Yale University Press, 1948).

Wesley Salmon, "Religion and Science: A New Look at Hume's *Dialogues*," *Philosophical Studies* 33(5) (1978): 143–176.

Robert Shope, *The Analysis of Knowing: A Decade of Research* (Princeton, NJ: Princeton University Press, 1983).

Jordan Howard Sobel, *Logic and Theism: Arguments For and Against Beliefs in God* (Cambridge: Cambridge University Press, 2009).

Richard Swinburne, *The Coherence of Theism*, 2nd edn (Oxford: Clarendon Press, 1993).

Richard Swinburne, *The Christian God* (Oxford: Oxford University Press, 1994).

Richard Swinburne, *The Existence of God*, rev. edn (Oxford: Oxford University Press, 2004).

Richard Swinburne, "Evidentialism," in Charles Taliaferro, Paul Draper, and Philip L. Quinn, eds, *A Companion to Philosophy of Religion*, 2nd edn (Malden, MA and Oxford: Wiley-Blackwell, 2010), pp. 681–688.

Paul Tillich, *Systematic Theology I* (Chicago, IL: University of Chicago Press, 1951).

Chris Tucker, "Satisficing and Motivated Submaximization (in the Philosophy of Religion)," *Philosophy and Phenomenological Research* (2015): doi: 10.1111/phpr.12191.

Jason Turner, "Compatibilism and the Free Will Defense," *Faith and Philosophy* 30(2) (2013): 125–137.

Peter van Inwagen, *The Problem of Evil* (Oxford: Oxford University Press, 2006).

Nicholas Wolterstorff, "Can Belief in God Be Rational If It Has No Foundations?," in Alvin Plantinga and Nicholas Wolterstorff, eds, *Faith and Rationality: Reason and Belief in God* (Notre Dame, IN: University of Notre Dame Press, 1983), pp. 135–186.

Erik Wielenberg, "Omnipotence Again," *Faith and Philosophy* 17(1) (2000): 26–47.

Edward Wierenga, "Review of James Tomberlin and Peter van Inwagen (eds.), *Alvin Plantinga*," *Faith and Philosophy* 5 (1988): 214–219.

Edward Wierenga, *The Nature of God: An Investigation into Divine Attributes* (Ithaca, NY: Cornell University Press, 1989).

Edward Wierenga, "Prophecy, Freedom, and the Necessity of the Past," *Philosophical Perspectives: Philosophy of Religion* 5 (1991): 425–445.

Edward Wierenga, "Timelessness out of Mind: On the Alleged Incoherence of Divine Timelessness," in Greg Ganssle and David Woodruff, eds, *God and Time* (Oxford: Oxford University Press, 2001), pp. 153–164.

Edward Wierenga, "Perfect Goodness and Divine Freedom," *Philosophical Books* 48(3) (2007): 207–216.

Edward Wierenga, "Omniscience," in Thomas Flint and Michael Rea, eds, *Oxford Handbook of Philosophical Theology* (Oxford: Oxford University Press, 2009): 129–144.

Edward Wierenga, "Augustinian Perfect Being Theology and the God of Abraham, Isaac, and Jacob," *International Journal for Philosophy of Religion* 69 (2011a): 139–151.

Edward Wierenga, "Tilting at Molinism," in Ken Perszyk, ed., *Molinism: The Contemporary Debate* (Oxford: Oxford University Press, 2011b), pp. 118–139.

Linda Zagzebski, "Divine Foreknowledge and Human Free Will," *Religious Studies* 21 (1985): 279–298.

Linda Zagzebski, "Religious Knowledge and the Virtues of the Mind," in Linda Zagzebski, ed., *Rational Faith: Catholic Responses to Reformed Epistemology* (Notre Dame, IN: University of Notre Dame Press, 1993), pp. 199–225.

Index

The Philosophy of Religion, First Edition. Edward R. Wierenga.
© 2016 Edward R. Wierenga. Published 2016 by John Wiley & Sons, Ltd.